P9-CFY-665

THE
STARS
IN
OUR EYES

ALSO BY JULIE KLAM

Please Excuse My Daughter

You Had Me at Woof

Love at First Bark

Friendkeeping

THE
STARS
IN
OUR EYES

*The Famous, the Infamous, and Why We
Care Way Too Much About Them*

★

JULIE KLAM

RIVERHEAD BOOKS
NEW YORK
2017

RIVERHEAD BOOKS
An imprint of Penguin Random House LLC
375 Hudson Street
New York, New York 10014

Library of Congress Cataloging-in-Publication Data

Names: Klam, Julie, author.
Title: The stars in our eyes : The famous, the infamous, and why we care way
too much about them / Julie Klam.
Description: New York : Riverhead Books, [2017]
Identifiers: LCCN 2016039409| ISBN 9781594631368 |
ISBN 9781101611180 (e-ISBN)
Subjects: LCSH: Fame. | Celebrities.
Classification: LCC BJ1470.5 .K49 2017 | DDC 306.4—dc23
LC record available at https://lccn.loc.gov/2016039409

Printed in the United States of America
1   3   5   7   9   10   8   6   4   2

BOOK DESIGN BY AMANDA DEWEY

*Penguin is committed to publishing works of quality and integrity.
In that spirit, we are proud to offer this book to our readers; however, the
story, the experiences, the opinions, and the words are the author's alone.*

For Dan

The more scribbled the name, the bigger the fame.

RUPERT PUPKIN,
The King of Comedy

CONTENTS

★

INTRODUCTION

Fade In

★

One summer evening, I was sitting in my bed watching *Rear Window*, a favorite movie of mine. I've seen it a million times, and each time I view it, the same thoughts occur to me: "God, Grace Kelly is so beautiful. She really is so perfect. Who would wear that dress to their boyfriend's apartment to make dinner?" As I watched, I Googled pictures of Grace on my phone and looked at photos of her wedding to Prince Rainier. My then eleven-year-old daughter, Violet, came into the room with her laptop and plunked down next to me.

"Mom, you have to watch this. It is so funny!" It was her current favorite YouTuber, Tyler Oakley. At that moment, he was the biggest star in her world, this guy filming himself in his basement (or his jail cell or whatever locale he's in). And I said to my daughter in my best old Jewy tone, "This is a star?"

The concept of celebrity and fame has changed enormously over time. Once it was Julius Caesar and Cleopatra. Now it's some woman on Instagram who does nude yoga and has 3.5 million followers, a thirteen-year-old "Viner," and a Korean rapper who posts videos that are viewed millions of times. So today who is a celebrity? And who gets to be a celebrity? Part of the answer to these questions seems to be "anyone with internet access." But there's more to it more than that.

This is what I'm here to explore: what celebrity means, why we care so much, why I care so much, and why you probably do, too. I believe that if we more clearly understand celebrity, if we can get a handle on our relationship to celebrity, we can better understand ourselves. And while I'm not a scientist or a researcher, I happen to be uniquely qualified to write this book: I've been writing it my whole life.

I've been enamored of celebrities for as long as I've been conscious of TV and movies and records and sports. And my definition of "celebrity" always has stretched pretty wide. The guy who played piano at the restaurant where our family used to have dinner when I was a kid? I got his autograph. (His name was Mack Leonard, and he signed the sheet music for his original song "Don't Take Me Anyplace but Poughkeepsie.") He was a celebrity to me. His autograph hung on my wall right next to a tiny, framed autograph from *Today* show film critic Gene Shalit, whose autograph I also got in one of my first forays into celebrity stalking. I had the autographs of my aunt Mattie's neighbor Christina, who was the model in the Enjoli TV commercial that went "I can bring home the bacon, fry it up in a pan, and never let you forget you're a man," and of a woman, Linda, who rode horses at the stable I took lessons at. She was in a Secret deodorant commercial. And in 1976, when our local Carvel ice-cream store grandly reopened with appearances from some of the lesser cast members of the Broadway musical *Grease*, I brought my autograph book and procured Doody's signature.

So I know about celebrity.

When I was young, I was convinced celebrities could save me. I was a middling (OK, below-average) student in school, not pretty or popular, occasionally teased. I was miserable. And it seemed to me that popularity and celebrity went together. The popular kids in my school were like our celebrities, because we all wanted to look at them and be around them, and even dress like them. So when Melissa Plechavicius started wearing a slim braid on the right side of her long, loose hair, we all followed her. When she switched to the left, so did we. Maybe if I knew a "real" celebrity, I remember thinking, people would emulate my 'do.

In 2006, I saw a music video while at the gym. (Well, "music" might be pushing it—it was Paris Hilton singing.) In the video an adorable tweenage boy is being bullied in school and suffers the classic humiliation of having his fully loaded lunch tray flipped in the cafeteria by one of the school meanies. Demoralized, he comes home to his bedroom, which is plastered with pictures of his favorite "singer," Paris Hilton. A moving van and Porsche pull up in front of the house next door, in a nice *Risky Business*–style suburban neighborhood. Out of the truck comes furniture that's being moved in next door. And who comes out of the car? What? It's PARIS HILTON? Gee, I wouldn't think of her as living in suburbia, but there you have it. The bullied boy's dog comes running out of his house and approaches Paris's adorable little pup, and Paris smiles. "Cute dog," she says to him, charmed by the idea that this young fan with boundary issues is her new next-door neighbor. Cut to the tweenage boy bringing the dazzling Ms. Hilton into the lunchroom with him. All the bullies are stunned, their jaws drop, and it isn't long before the main bully's own lunch tray is flipped exactly the way our hero's was earlier in the video. The young boy is a victor. With her amazing superpower—celebrity—Paris has turned a loser into a winner and saved the day.

And scene.

I have to admit I watched the video every time it came on, despite having to listen to her sing. I was fascinated by its message even as I mocked it. Not because of Paris Hilton, whose celebrity status is questionable at best. We no longer seem to require that people's fame be attached to anything other than renown. (Cough, Kardashians, cough.)

But the video's message struck a chord with me. I, too, had been a dorky kid who fantasized about bringing a movie star to school. In my case it was *Blue Lagoon* heartthrob Christopher Atkins. For those of you who don't remember, *The Blue Lagoon* was a very big summer movie in 1980, when I was thirteen. It stars Brooke Shields and Christopher Atkins as blond, supertan, quasi-incestuous cousins. It takes place on a tropical island in the South Pacific, and the actors wear very little clothing. It's fabulous. My friends and I *loved* it—we loved Brooke and really loved Chris. (That I call him Chris is one of the effects of his being a celebrity: people you've never met and probably never will meet call you by your first name, or nickname, in casual conversation with readers you also will probably never meet.)

It just so happened that Chris was the nephew of close friends of my parents'. My mother had even gone to a prescreening of the movie with her friend Patty. Christopher Atkins was there and signed a poster for me while I was in school, failing math, cutting bangs to cover my forehead zits, running last in gym on the track behind the girl with crutches, and generally mastering the arts of unpopularity and awkwardness. It was the end of eighth grade, and the school was going to be throwing a dance in the cafeteria. That was when I had my genius idea. Christopher Atkins would be my date to the dance! Just like the kid in the Paris Hilton video, I would walk into the cafeteria on his arm, his white teeth and perfect blond hair almost as stunning as my Lanz of Salzburg white eyelet dress and Stridex-ad complexion, and suddenly my life would change. I'd be . . . a STAH! No more looking around the cafeteria for a seat—someone would be holding it for me and would have brought in my lunch from the 21 Club like Grace Kelly did for Jimmy Stewart in *Rear Window*.

I obsessed about it for weeks, and probably even shared the exciting news with a few of my closest friends. Then I was told that he was overseas promoting *The Blue Lagoon*, by that time a big hit, and would not be able to come to my dance in the cafeteria. I wasn't heartbroken, though. I just thought it would give me time to set it up better for the following year, because the ninth-grade dance was at the Holiday Inn in Mount Kisco! So much more elegant than our cafeteria.

Chris didn't take me to that one, either, but by then I'd moved on to more hard-core celebrity crushes. Angsty Timothy Hutton, bad boy Sean Penn, Kevin Bacon, Mel Gibson in *The Road Warrior,* Tom Cruise. And I didn't just plaster my room with their posters; I traveled into Manhattan alone in a blizzard on a Sunday afternoon to see Sean Penn and Kevin Bacon in an off-Broadway play (one row and one degree from Mr. Bacon).

At that point in my life most of my knowledge of celebrities came from teen magazines (*Tiger Beat, Teen Beat, Seventeen*) and *People* magazine, and the occasional *Entertainment Tonight* segment. When I loved Richard Gere in *An Officer and a Gentleman,* I went to my local candy store and bought a copy of *Jet* magazine with Louis Gossett Jr. on the cover. I was desperate for any information and pictures to put on my wall, and those were my resources. Can you imagine that today? It's like I grew up in the Sahara of celebrity news and am now living under Niagara Falls. Today all of us have unlimited access to every famous—or infamous—person's life. There was no internet then with a billion gossip sites, no TV channels devoted to twenty-four-hour breaking celebrity stories, no *Behind the Music,* no actresses tweeting stills from their self-produced sex tapes. Today it's gotten to a point of near madness. In 2015 Alec Baldwin came out fists swinging and said the paparazzi, those photographers who captured the images we so eagerly devour, were endangering his family. He said that paparazzi can "make life miserable for my neighbors," and there's nothing that authorities can do about it. Photographers "provoke me, daily, by getting dangerously close to me with their cameras as weapons, hoping I will react," Baldwin wrote. "When I do, the weapon doubles as a device to record my reaction." He goes on to offer a theory of why Americans are so interested in celebrities:

"This country's obsession with the private lives of famous people is tragic. It's tragic in the sense that it is so clearly a projection of people's frustration about their government, their economy, their own spiritual bankruptcy. You have no voice in Washington. In Washington, or in any statehouse, no one actually cares what you think. So you post online, you vote with a Romanesque thumbs up or down on the celebrity debacle of the day. That is your right. It's also fatal misdirection of your voice and need to judge. Occupy Wall Street, on their worst day, had more integrity than the comments page of [a] website ever will."

OK, I understand what Baldwin is saying. But what about the Instagram feed of his wife, Hilaria? Selfie after selfie of her doing bizarre yoga poses with her babies for all the world to see (or at least her 205,000 followers). No one was clamoring for that. Celebrity is a choice you can't have both ways.

In the end, Baldwin says he may have to leave acting altogether. "If quitting the television business, the movie business, the theatre, any component of entertainment, is necessary in order to bring safety and peace to my family, then that is an easy decision." So far that doesn't seem to have happened: As I write this, the website IMDb lists at least ten movie and television projects that Baldwin is involved in, including producing a TV reboot of *Match Game*, which may be one of the most celebrity-focused game shows of all time.

So it's clear that famous people aren't all thrilled with this new world of celebrity.

I know my mother's generation had a very different retrieval system for their celebrity gossip. They read newspapers to learn about their favorite sports stars and bought "movie" magazines with carefully orchestrated features about the biggest celebrities, with all the information coming from studio publicists. And it wasn't just the articles about the stars; their lives were controlled as well. Though Katharine Hepburn carried on a famous love affair with the married Spencer Tracy, that was kept out of the news.

Today's stars, whether they're actors or athletes or politicians, are in charge of their own lives. They can do what they want. And so we think we know them better when we see them behaving "just like us." They squeeze their own mangoes in the grocery store, they push their own kids on the swings at the park, they drink the same grande soy macchiatos with one pump of hazelnut that we do. OMG! JUST LIKE US!!!

We watch Julia Louis-Dreyfus talk shopping to Jerry Seinfeld's wife and maybe think, "I shop online! I know what that's like!" Or Chris Rock talking to David Letterman about the Mets, and you also complain about the Mets. Or Tom Cruise is acting nutty on *Oprah*, and you think, "Gee, I've jumped on a couch." (OK, maybe not that.) But somehow these snapshots make us feel that we know these famous people, that we understand what their lives are like, even a little bit, and that their lives are not so different from the non-celebrity ones we live.

Except when I buy a mango or a cup of coffee, or my kid has a temper tantrum in the middle of Amsterdam Avenue, there isn't a herd of photographers snapping away. I'm not trying to look normal and as if no one's watching me. I *am* normal and no one *is* watching me. It rarely makes the nightly news when I leave my home without makeup or buy my kid an ice cream before dinner or dare to wear a bathing suit when I've clearly gained five pounds. And when I broke up with my husband, I was able to deal with it privately, as opposed to the lovely Jennifer Garner, who needed to address her breakup with Ben Affleck in *Vanity Fair*, and Ben Affleck, who needed to respond to her *Vanity Fair* interview in a *New York Times* article.

Imagine that for a minute. You and your partner—one or both of you famous the world over—break up, which, no matter who you are, is extraordinarily painful. Not only must you deal with your pain, and possibly your children's pain, but also people who don't know you and have never met you feel comfortable writing about it and you and speculating about the causes, your personality flaws, and the answers to problems that are no one's but yours. Editors at magazines or websites find a picture of you taken in the middle of a sneeze and say it was you bursting into tears at the sight of your beloved and his paramour and publish it or post it on their sites.

That's when I find myself in long conversations with strangers about Jen's bravery and Ben's cad-ery. And I know I'm one of millions.

I was in line at the grocery store in March 2016 and Jennifer Garner's *Vanity Fair* cover story was on the stands, and the woman behind me said, "Of course it was his fault! That's just what he did to JLo." I nodded so as not to seem rude, but I don't actually remember what broke up Bennifer; I just remember I wasn't that interested in them. I watched them be interviewed together on a television special or something, and I remember thinking they had no chemistry—that they were unconvincing and unreal and not suited for each other. (Just because I wasn't interested in them does not mean I don't have an opinion about them or can't pass judgment on them. That's one of the great advantages of having celebrities: They're so well-known you can tell everyone what you think of them, and not only do people *not* judge you for that, but they have an opinion on them, too!)

I don't think any of us really knows how it would feel to live under the microscope like that—to have people who don't know you love you or hate you or worship you or blame you. That must be extremely difficult to handle.

What might it feel like to be famous? It depends. But one constant seems to be that normal people get indignant and insolent about the behavior of a celebrity when it doesn't coincide with their expectations. In 2016 Amy Schumer declared she wouldn't allow any more fan photos when a guy demanded one, saying, "It's America and we paid for you." Some people act like it's their right to interact with a famous person; it's like how a taxpayer feels about the police, or a British person feels about Queen Elizabeth. "If you didn't want photographers shoving their cameras in your faces, why did you choose to be an actor/athlete/politician/queen?" people ask. Well, one answer to that question is that most celebrities didn't know what it would be like either. They followed their dreams, and after a lot of hard work and a bit of luck, they achieved them. But they didn't realize that the ceaseless laser beam of celebrity would be one of the consequences of that success, acclaim, and popularity. They didn't know how little control they would have over their own lives once they realized their dream.

When a person wants to become, say, an actor, she prepares. She takes a monologue workshop and scene-study, improvisation, Shakespeare, movement, and voice classes. She does Pilates to keep her body looking good and gets an expensive haircut. She learns how to perform on a stage and in front of a camera. She goes on auditions, watches other actors perform, and lives and breathes acting. This is how she prepares for her career. The one class no school offers, however, is how to prepare yourself for when you're on the cover of *Star* magazine with a black bar across your eyes and under the headline "GUESS WHO THE WORST BIKINI BODY BELONGS TO?"

My friend Isabel Gillies, a writer and actress, has given me a glimpse into this world. She played Kathy Stabler, the wife of Elliot Stabler, who was played by Christopher Meloni on *Law and Order: Special Victims Unit.*

"I'm not *famous* famous, but I was on *Law and Order: SVU* for twelve years," she says. "I get recognized for that a lot. Sometimes when someone recognizes me, they look mad. I think it's because they know they've seen me somewhere before, but they're not sure. And because I'm insecure, their who-is-that face reads to me as mad. Once I was in a sporting goods store, and someone working behind the cash register was giving me one of those faces. I started to panic, thinking I was in the wrong place or I had stolen something. Then someone else behind the counter figured out I was on *Law and Order.* Then everyone got happy, and we all had a thirty-second party and somebody took a selfie."

When my daughter was in kindergarten, my then husband and I switched her to another school about a month into the year. She and I were both nervous about the new people there. One day after I dropped her off, one of the mothers asked me to go out for coffee. As we sat in a diner near the school, I realized she was Caitlin Abramovitz, a *Seventeen* model I had worshipped when I was young. I knew her story from the magazine: She had been discovered roller skating in Central Park. Though she (and Isabel, who had also been a teen model in New York City) are still drop-dead gorgeous, Caitlin hasn't modeled since she was a kid.

I was clearly more caught up in this realization than she was. I asked her about it and absorbed all her stories about traveling to islands with the big teen models of the time, like Phoebe Cates and Lisanne Falk (who was an actress, too, and appeared in *Heathers*), who taught her how to shave her legs and walk.

Both Caitlin and Isabel are smart, funny, confident, self-deprecating women. So I was surprised when Isabel admitted: "Modeling was a short-lived career for me, as I wasn't great at it. But the first job I got was the cover of *Seventeen* magazine. Everyone, including me, was like, whoa. It gave me a little peek at what it would be like to be famous, because everyone in my age group read *Seventeen*. My agent put me in my place right away. One day I was sauntering around the office as if I were Paulina Porizkova, and he asked, 'You having fun being the most famous person on your block this week?'"

This was a fate I could only imagine: having your picture everywhere at the age when most girls are at the apex of their hideous awkwardness. Listening to Isabel made me realize there are all different types of fame and celebrity. There are people who are famous in their fields but who can't get a reservation at

Orso. (If you don't know what Orso is, then you're not plugged into the celebrity matrix. OK, I'll tell you: It's a restaurant in New York. And the actress Doris Roberts told me a story about how she could walk in there anytime and get a table while she was starring in *Everybody Loves Raymond*, but a couple of years after that, she walked in and they said they were all booked. She looked at her companion and said, "When you're hot you're hot, when you're not, you're not" and went elsewhere.)

There are famous people who have extraordinary and specific talents, like professional athletes and musicians who play one instrument brilliantly. There are politicians, well-known for their thoughtful views on issues of national importance. And then there are people who are famous because of their unflinching desire to be famous (and you know who they are . . . our friend Paris Hilton).

To paraphrase the famous quote, some people are born to fame (Prince George, Blue Ivy), some achieve fame (Meryl Streep, Colin Firth), and some have fame thrust upon them (those who survive a plane crash). How do all these different people deal with fame? Do they ever wish they could turn it off? When it goes away, are they sad?

These are the questions I want answers to.

I once heard a story on NPR about a neurobiologist at Duke University Medical Center. In 2005, Dr. Michael Platt led what I thought was a fascinating experiment with twelve adult male rhesus macaque monkeys. He gave the macaques some salty snacks, making them thirsty, then offered them a choice: their favorite drink (in this case cherry Juicy Juice) or the opportunity to look at pictures of their group's dominant "celebrity" monkeys, the ones with the power and magnetism. All the monkeys chose the photos. The desire to look at this celebrity monkey was so strong that it supplanted thirst.

But these macaques weren't willing to give up the juice to look at pictures of subordinate monkeys, Platt found. In fact, they had to be bribed with extra juice to watch the rhesus B-list.

And it turned out that the "celebrity" monkeys were just as interested in their fellow celebrity monkeys as the others were.

If we are anything like these monkeys, our human desire for and attraction to fame seem hardwired in primates in surprising ways. (I'm convinced this explains why I saw a very famous actress at my hair salon reading *Us Weekly*, because NATURE!)

So, my fellow B-list monkeys, I invite you to join me as I try to uncover the enduring magic of these earthly stars.

ONE

WHAT WE TALK ABOUT WHEN WE TALK ABOUT CELEBRITIES

★

The 20th-century comedian Fred Allen says in his book *Treadmill to Oblivion* that "a celebrity is a person who works hard all his life to become known, then wears dark glasses to avoid being recognized."

Ta-Nehisi Coates, a wonderful writer whose book *Between the World and Me* exploded when it was published in 2015 and turned him into a literary celebrity, was devastated to see that when he bought a brownstone in Brooklyn, its address, the price he paid for it, and his move-in date were printed in the New York newspapers. "It is true what they say about celebrity—people suddenly don't quite see you," he wrote in the *Atlantic*. "You walk into a room and you are not a person, so much as symbol of whatever someone needs you to be." The attention was so great, he announced, that he and his family wouldn't move into the building after all.

There are all kinds of fame. You can be famous in one realm while in another no one knows who you are. I have an astrophysicist friend who every so often blows a gasket because he met Dr. Hecklemeyer Doofenberger. *The* Dr. Hecklemeyer Doofenberger. It's the same thing with writers. Famous writers (with the possible exceptions of Stephen King and James Patterson) are not necessarily household names. But that's one of the cool aspects of celebrity: you don't have to be Madonna; you don't have to be famous to everyone to be famous.

Since the dawn of the dinosaurs, celebrity has been a thing. OK, maybe not the dinosaurs (unless you count Stony Curtis from *The Flintstones, which I do*). In civilizations across the centuries, we would probably classify Queen Nefertiti, Cleopatra, those Russell Crowe–type gladiators, Julius Caesar, and Jesus as early celebrities. The rumors about Genghis Khan and Henry VIII and Marie Antoinette and Rasputin were as titillating to their kingdoms as the latest Kardashian nude selfie is to our world. When movies became popular early in the 20th century, we made international celebrities of performers like Mary Pickford, Charlie Chaplin, and Rudolph Valentino (swoon!). Our politicians have been famous for as long as there have been governments, and in our time some of them have gained celebrity status, such as when John Kennedy hung out with Marilyn Monroe. At the dawn of radio, professional athletes—including Babe Ruth, Lou Gehrig, and Joe Louis—who'd been known for their exploits on the playing fields or boxing rings only through newspapers assumed newfound notoriety. So did singers and musicians, from Bing Crosby to Elvis to Aretha Franklin to the Beatles and the Rolling Stones. When television started appearing in average Americans' houses in the middle of the 1950s, performers like Lucille Ball, Milton Berle, and Jackie Gleason became household faces. And as the number of entertainment outlets grew—from TV to cable TV to premium channels to Netflix and Hulu to on-demand movies to billions of websites from all around the world, now anyone with an iPhone and a less-than-normal amount of shame can be famous.

Which brings me to the moment when I start to explain this book to people.

"So, what exactly is this book about?" Griffin Dunne asks.

He is across the table from me at a café near his apartment in SoHo, one of New York City's chicest—and most celebrity-filled—neighborhoods. He's in his late 50s but could pass for twenty years younger, and is completely adorable in an Allman Brothers *Eat a Peach* T-shirt and baseball cap.

Looking at this bona fide famous person, an actor/producer/director who actually knows Madonna—MADONNA—demands all my attention. His dad, Dominick Dunne, was in show business, too, and Griffin has lived around fame since he was in footy pajamas and a bathrobe. He understands it.

"It's about the nature of celebrity," I say.

He frowns and furrows his brow. I know that look. Timothy Hutton had it a few months before, as did pretty much everyone else I talked to about this book. Because they're thinking: "What are you *talking about*, girl who wrote some books about dogs and friends and your mother, and how did I get roped into this conversation?"

"Who else have you talked to?" Griffin asks, trying to see if perhaps my earlier research will make this clearer. This sort of suspicion or wariness from celebrities is something I'm getting accustomed to. They need to be careful about what they say on the record: They're not like those of us who freely talk politics with strangers on the subway, whose words are not headlines. Celebrity is both a reward for a job well done and a weapon to destroy someone's privacy, reputation, and chance at a normal life.

"Timothy Hutton, Denis Leary, Michael Black, Adam Schweitzer, Julie Warner, Doris Roberts . . . ," I begin, rattling off an impressive list.

"And what did you tell them to get them to talk to you?"

Oh my God. I want to run away with my giant New York City PS 87 tote bag filled with a pumpkin bread I baked for him, as well as signed copies of some of my books. Why did I bring these things with me? Because I'm not a journalist. David Frost didn't bring Richard Nixon a Bundt cake when he interviewed him in 1977. No. Pumpkin loaves are for amateurs.

"Well, uh, they talked to me because, um, I knew people who knew them." I say. "Not Timothy Hutton, though. I know him."

"Oh, how do you know Tim?" Griffin asks, desperate to grasp at something to explain why he's sitting here with me.

"I, um, met him on Twitter," I say.

Griffin, I learn, is not on Twitter. He doesn't understand how I got to "know" a great, Academy Award–winning actor through social media.

"Blech, Twitter. I can't wait for it to just go away," he says.

I try to explain the benefits of Twitter, and as I speak I can hear myself becoming one of the people I used to pass every morning standing outside the ABC building that housed the *Live with Regis and Kathie Lee* show. Five or six oddballs with autograph books came every morning to wait and get signatures from whatever guest was desperately darting from the building into their waiting limousine post-interview. Now that was me, the real-life Sandra Bernhard in *The King of Comedy* (though in my defense I wasn't asking for autographs).

"But now we're real-life friends, Tim and I." I say "Tim" because his real-life friends don't call him Timothy.

Griffin doesn't look as if he believes me.

I think back to when I wrote my first book and people would ask me what it was about. I would start stuttering and then try to remember the flap copy: "Julie Klam was raised as the only daughter of one of the three Jewish families in the exclusive WASP stronghold of Bedford, New York. Her mother was something, her father was something else, and she ended up somehow turning it into a book?" All I can think now is how bad I am at explaining whatever it is I'm trying to do, but I know why. It's just kind of embarrassing to explain to Griffin. (We are friends now, so I call him Griffin, instead of Mr. Dunne. Any day now, though, I might switch to Griff.)

In my desperation I look across the table at Griffin, and I think—I hope—that he is starting to understand what I want to know from him and what I'm trying to write about. Or maybe he just hopes to get back home to his beautiful apartment and gorgeous wife before the sun sets.

Why do we feel this way about celebrities—people we've never met? Why did my eighty-six-year-old grandfather when reading the *Miami Herald* once bark, "I hate Johnny Depp!"? I tell Griffin that by talking to the celebrities themselves about the concept of celebrity, I will better understand this relationship—what they're putting out, what we are getting back.

Griffin still doesn't look completely convinced. So I give it one more shot.

"A few years ago," I say, "my husband and I split up."

Griffin nods.

"My daughter, who was then nine years old, was watching me going through some legal papers, and she saw her name and asked why she was in there. I explained that a lot of our divorce had to do with how her father and I could take care of her the best way possible. She suddenly got teary-eyed and asked me who would take care of her if something happened to me and her dad. I explained to her that now that we didn't live together, it was very unlikely that something would happen to us at the same time. She wasn't satisfied. I told her that years before, our plan was for her to live with one of her aunts and uncle, but now that she was a bit older, she could have a say in whom she lived with.

"She sat and thought for a couple of minutes and finally said, 'OK, I choose Seth Meyers.'"

Griffin laughs. I remark, "It's funny, but she's only thirteen, so he is still on the hook for another five years."

Without me saying anything more, he gets what I'm after.

Intermission 1

If you're a writer, people always ask you what you're working on. Most of the time, I tell them (a dog book, a friendship column), and they nod and move on. Doing research for this book, however, I noticed something remarkable: just about every person I mentioned it to told me a story of a celebrity encounter. What I found—and continue to find—is that people vividly recall a sometimes-brief interaction that might have taken place forty years ago. They may not remember a second of their time in fourth grade, but they remember seeing Paul Newman putting gas in his Datsun that summer. That distinction is important to me—poignant and human. I obviously think a lot about celebrities and see them as significant. And I wanted to hear the celebrity stories that have affected others, so I decided to ask a large swath of people about brushes with celebrities that meant something to them, and I included them in this book. (The bios of those who shared their stories can be found in the back of this book.)

It must have been more than twenty-five years ago I spotted Audrey Hepburn on the men's floor at Saks Fifth Avenue. She was easy to spot because she was wearing a belted trench coat, big sunglasses, and one of those tiny scarves tied around that perfect head. I was shopping for a birthday present for my brother-in-law, so it must have been in May. I couldn't help myself; I started to follow her around the store.

First she bought a cashmere sweater (for a man) and so did I. My brother-in-law loved that I bought the same one she bought. She started to look through a table of shirts but didn't buy any. Me neither. Then she took the escalator down to the first floor and started to browse the makeup counters. No one recognized her! It was lunchtime, and I was late, so I left her to fend for herself. OK, it was a little bit of stalking, BUT IT WAS AUDREY HEPBURN!

—ESTHER NEWBERG

★

Several years ago I was waiting in a small lobby where a friend of mine, Nancy Ringham, was performing. The place was very crowded, and there wasn't a lot of room to mingle. I'm standing there talking to somebody else when an old man just plows through the crowd, pushing me out of his way. That's not the kind of behavior I put with—from any-body; I have a real scorn for people with bad manners. So I turned around and said, "Hey!" That got his attention. So this old man turned around and looked straight at me. It was Rex Harrison. Henry Fucking Higgins. He didn't say a word—no apology, no acknowledgment, nothing. To him, I was just young and I was in his way. He clearly thought I was less than nothing. So I called him an "old man." Loudly.

—MARY TESTA

TWO

CHILD STARS

The Good, the Bad, and the Ugly

★

There are monumental differences in celebrities having to do with what time in their lives they became famous. Someone who became a star at age forty-five, say, has a very different perspective on celebrity than someone who got their start in Gerber baby food commercials. I wanted to find out what it was like to grow up in the business from someone who lived through it. So I talked to the first child celebrity I remember vividly: Quinn Cummings.

I first saw Quinn in 1977. I was eleven; she was ten. She was on a movie screen; I was in a movie seat.

I had gone into New York City to spend the weekend with my aunt Mattie, and after one of the finest cheeseburger deluxes and Cokes I'd ever tasted in my eleven years on this planet, we went to the Sutton movie theater on 57th Street to see *The Goodbye Girl*.

Aunt Mattie bought tickets and we went to get popcorn. But no. To my shock, there was no popcorn. Instead, the concession stand was stocked with home-baked goods. Giant chocolate-chip cookies, slices of pink cakes, fruit tarts, and the huge dark-chocolate brownie that I selected.

(I know I loved *The Goodbye Girl*, but as God is my witness, I never see anything associated with that movie without thinking, "Mmmm, brownie . . .")

When I admitted this to the now grown-up Quinn Cummings, she was gracious. "I'm so happy to be associated with any baked good."

We became acquainted several years ago when she published a book edited by a friend of mine, who introduced us because she thought we would like each other. We emailed and didn't meet in person until a few years later, and by that time I was as huge a fan of her writing as I was of her acting (brownie). From what I saw, she was a well-adjusted, healthy, down-to-earth, smart, decent, generous, animal-rescuing woman, and a very attentive mother. In short, she's not a clichéd damaged grown-up child star. I also didn't get the impression that Quinn was excited to be talking about her former career, but she was doing it to help me (see: generous).

As someone who has interviewed famous people for more than twenty years, I knew what questions to ask, but I also knew she'd been asked them eight zillion times. As much as I wanted her insider's glimpse into celebrity, I also wanted Quinn not to hate this discussion, or me. So I took a deep breath and said, "I know you've been asked this, but I'm still curious: How do you think you escaped being a child-star casualty?"

"My mother raised a human being, not a movie star," Quinn said crisply.

I apologized. It must be annoying to be asked why you didn't turn out to be a big failure, a loser, a junkie, or dead, or have your own church.

"I could've had my own church?" Quinn chuckled. "Missed opportunity."

Quinn Cummings, I learned, began acting in 1975 at the age of eight with small parts in TV shows like *The Six Million Dollar Man*. She was then cast in *The Goodbye Girl* and was nominated for an Oscar and a Golden Globe as best supporting actress for her role as Lucy, Marsha Mason's irrepressible daughter. She then went on to co-star in the television series *Family* and did cameos here and there (including on *The Love Boat*, the jewel in any cameo crown) and by the 1990s pretty much stopped acting.

Quinn credits her successful maneuvering through a busy childhood to caring parents, but it was more than that. Her mother was on a Screen Actors Guild committee to improve conditions for child actors. It was convened in response to the 1939 Coogan Law. Jackie Coogan was one of the biggest child stars of the early 20th century, after co-starring in Charlie Chaplin's *The Kid* and winning fans; his likeness graced truckloads of memorabilia and merchandise, even jars of peanut butter. It wasn't until he turned twenty-one that Coogan realized he didn't have any of the money he made when he was a child.

The 1920s were the start of child labor laws, but there was nothing about the earnings of a minor. At the time, the money a child made simply belonged to the parents.

Coogan sued his mother and former manager, and as a result, in 1939, a California law was passed to protect the kids. Dubbed the Coogan Law, its goal was to keep future young performers from losing their earnings. The 1939 incarnation of the Coogan Law wasn't perfect—there were loopholes in the law that some people took advantage of—and people on the actors' union committees, including Quinn's mother, tried to close them.

"So the money I made as an actor went to pay for my college education, my house, and my freedom," Quinn said.

Listening to Quinn describe how her mother kept the money she had made in a trust for her, I started thinking about stage mothers. I remember working in New York's theater district in the 1990s, and one day I was eating lunch at an Irish pub when a woman, frumpy and hard looking, came in with a little girl who looked to be about five years old. The child was dressed in an elegant red wool coat with a black fur collar and a matching beret, her hair in two perfect sandy braids fastened with velvet bows. On her face was an expression of pure misery.

"I'm hungry," she whined.

The woman—who turned out to be her mother—told the girl that she would get her some french fries, but it had to be quick because they were already running late for the audition. The woman ordered the fries from the waitress and began giving directions to the girl. The child wasn't allowed to take off her coat or get anything on her face. And then the woman looked at her and said, "I've done your hair, worked hard to pay for your new outfit, taught you the lines . . . Now I can't do any more. The rest is up to you."

The rest. Is up. To you. To you, five-year-old kid who looks like she wants to be here about as much as the guy swishing the mop over the beer-soaked floor. The scene was depressing: a disappointed woman pinning her desires for fame and fortune—for celebrity—on her kid. A small person who was hungry and unhappy. And then, bummer of all bummers: the fries took too long to be served. The mother looked at her watch, snatched the kid's arm, and left. Now the waitress was unhappy, too.

The classic overbearing stage parent like Brooke Shields's mother, Teri, is the one we tend to think most about, but all the people I know whose children are performers are lovely. And in all those cases, the desire to act or sing is driven by the child, not the parent. From what I saw that day in the theater district, this was not the case here. It caused me to wonder: Is that any worse than a parent who pushes their kids into sports they don't want to play? Well, yes. For one thing, children don't earn money playing youth soccer.

I spoke to my friend Deborah Copaken about this. Her son Jacob Kogan was a child actor. It wasn't ever her dream. It was his—even at age four. While my preschool dreams involved edible paste, his were up on the silver screen.

"To avoid paying for music classes, I started a baby music class. I played the guitar and we sang," Deb told me. "I did it with a group of friends. We got together at my place on Monday nights. One of the people in the group was a friend of a friend who was a casting agent, and she was casting a Lasse Hallström movie. Jacob, who was four, would show up at the music class, reading. 'He reads?' she said to me. 'Yeah, he taught himself to read.' The woman said she needed a really young kid who can memorize lines who looks like him." The casting agent asked Deb if she'd bring him in for an audition.

"I wasn't crazy about him being an actor," Deb said. "But it was Lasse Hallström, who was really cool. Jacob has a photographic memory, so he looked at the lines and memorized them. We brought him in and he nailed the audition. It was down to Jacob and a six-year-old, and they decided they'd rather have a six-year-old than a four-year-old. And Jacob said, 'OK, when's my next audition?' And I said no, that was it. And he said he really wanted to be in a movie. I said, 'It's a lot of work for you, and I would have to take you to these auditions.' In the meantime, Paul [her ex-husband] gets a videotape in the mail. It was a movie he had been in as a kid in Russia. His mom was a refusenik and she'd lost her job, so Paul and his twin brother worked, and they appeared in a movie to help pay the rent. Jacob watched it and said, 'Well, Dad was an actor. Why can't I be one?'"

Deb just kept putting him off. "So now three years have gone by, he's seven, still asking. I signed him up for acting classes, musical theater classes, and he still just wants to audition. I talked to a friend of mine who was a child psychiatrist and asked what to do. She said one of the reasons so many child actors get fucked up is because they are living out the fantasies of the parents. It's the parents who want to be famous. That's not the case here—this is what *he* wants to do—so let him try it.

"My daughter, Sasha, who is a year younger than Jacob, had a friend in her kindergarten class who was an actress, and her mother gave us the name of her agent. I involved Jacob in the process. I said we need to mail a letter and some pictures, so pick three pictures out of the photo album. He did and I wrote a letter that basically said, 'My son wants to be an actor, I think it's a super bad idea, but if you can convince us otherwise, here are three pictures of him.'"

The agent loved Deb's letter and called her. She and Jacob met with the agent, and the agent wanted to sign Jacob. He started going out on auditions in New York and worked in the theater and in commercials all through his childhood. That was fifteen years ago. Today, Jacob is a college student and still performs. While he never achieved the success or the fame that Quinn Cummings did, he did play young Spock in J.J. Abrams's 2009 film *Star Trek* and managed to maintain his sanity as a child actor and as an adult.

The sad truth is that when I was young I would've *loved* to have become a child actress. Looking back, I was fortunate to have neither the talent nor the looks, so that at no time was this a serious potentiality to anyone but me in my vivid imagination. Growing up I had a dressing table with a three-sided mirror in my bedroom, and if I leaned a certain way, I thought my reflection was kind of drop-dead gorgeous (though my profile in the same pose made me look like Margaret Hamilton as Almira Gulch in *The Wizard of Oz*, but I would know that wasn't my good side).

Child actors aren't famous only in the movies or on television. Like a million other little girls, I saw *Annie*, the pinnacle of child-star success, on Broadway—many times. (This, of course, was before tickets for Broadway musicals cost a second mortgage.) I thought no one in the world was luckier than the kids who played those orphans. I don't think I ever wanted to be Annie. I just wanted one of the smaller roles; there were fewer lines to memorize. (Always keeping the bar low, that's me.) The experience of performing and having people watching you felt like magic to me as a kid. I didn't imagine how hard these kids worked or that there was a ton of daunting competition to get where they were, plus they were doing schoolwork on top of stage work. I imagined they just stepped out of a cab a few minutes before 3 o'clock (I was a matinee kid), put on their costume, walked out onto the stage when the orchestra started the overture, got loud laughs and standing ovations, and then went home to their glamorous apartments and movie-star friends and hot-fudge sundaes.

Maybe because I was their age when the first production of *Annie* ran on Broadway, the performers in *Annie* always felt like "it"—the biggest deal to me. I saw my first *Annie*, with the amazing Andrea McArdle, when I was eleven, then I saw it twice more with Shelley Bruce. (I saw it again in college with my aunt, and then I saw it *again* with my daughter.) I hadn't thought of Shelley Bruce in a long time when I saw a comment she'd made on one of Quinn Cummings's Facebook statuses. So I friended her. And she accepted. That was a big thrill to me: an icon of my childhood as social media BFF (when BFF means person you don't know but are friends with on Facebook). I've never met her and didn't really interact with her, though I "liked" her posts of dog pictures. Whenever I did that, I had the feeling that I was doing it for sixth-grade Julie, the Julie who so wanted to be one of the girls who sang and danced behind her onstage at the Alvin Theatre eight times a week.

A while later I noticed that Alison Arngrim, who played Nellie Oleson on *Little House on the Prairie*, was Quinn's Facebook friend, too. Also Erin Murphy, who played Tabitha on *Bewitched*. I didn't friend them, but I wondered what was going on. I imagined Quinn and these other child actors being a version of Norma Desmond's "waxworks" in *Sunset Boulevard*. Remember the scene where Buster Keaton, Anna Q. Nilsson, and H. B. Warner all play bridge with her? Was there a secret club of not-fucked-up Hollywood child stars? And if there was, could I be their coffee girl and listen in on their conversations?

I asked Quinn about it in the least offensive way I could muster. And she gave me the background.

"Alison Arngrim and I grew up next door to one another for the first three years of my life; in fact, I have a picture of her at my third birthday party, where she is white-blond with many yards of legs, and I'm a bowling ball. I admire the work she's doing for abused children tremendously and am impressed that she's making being a former child actor into a nice paying gig. Not my idea of fun, but hey, if they're looking at you anyway, get paid.

"I sort of knew Mary McDonough [the girl who played Erin Walton on *The Waltons*], and she has a terrible picture of me at fourteen in her possession, which I have begged her never to reveal; if I had a less-attractive phase, I would prefer not to know about it. Perm, fat face, what appears to be a bowl haircut . . . I say no more.

"Kami Cotler [who played Elizabeth Walton] and I went to

prep school together. She was a couple of years ahead of me, so we weren't hugely close, but I admire her in the same way I admire Alison—just in the opposite direction: she got her master's from Berkeley, she's a charter school principal, she left acting behind without so much as a glance.

"Some of the other people who acted on my list are there because they're friends with Alison and they found me. Apparently I was always seen as the standoffish one, the one who didn't hang with them because . . . well, they weren't sure, what with me not being around to explain myself. I think it was a combination of my natural indifference to social interaction and my mother's drumbeat narrative that acting wasn't something I was, acting was something I did. I worked, and then I went home and hung out with the dog and the cat, who were, candidly, better company than many actors I knew, because even cats are less self-absorbed than actors."

Not as sordid as I imagined, this pod of grown-up child stars. And it was a relief to know that all of them seemed relatively OK, or as OK as non-child actors can be. It gave me hope that being famous as a child wasn't a psychological death sentence.

Quinn has a vivid metaphor for celebrity: "Great fame is kind of like that torture where you're in a room where they never turn the lights off," she said. "Thanks to phones and social media, there's no place where the famous person isn't fair game."

In the late 1990s, when I was working on the VH1 show *Pop-Up Video*, I had an assignment to "pop"—the term we use for inserting info-bubbles—a *Behind the Music* about Leif Garrett.

Over the years it's become kind of a famous episode because Leif was a beautiful teenybopper in the '70s. He was omnipresent on teen magazines during that time—truly a child superstar; maybe not the level of Justin Bieber, but right up there—when I was young. And then at some point the gossip was that he was living with Nicollette Sheridan, a child model and stepdaughter of Telly Savalas. The next time I was aware of Leif, we were both adults, and he had admitted to being a junkie and was in a serious car accident with a friend of his (described in the *Behind the Music* segment as a "promising young dancer") that had left the friend paralyzed. Leif had been in and out of rehab several times, and when he was interviewed for *Behind the Music,* he said he was clean. Well, it's possible that he'd just come from the dentist and had a lot of Novocain, but he seemed pretty out of it to me. When I watched it—and I watched it over and over— I wondered, if Leif had had a "normal" childhood, how would the rest of his life have turned out? He clearly had addiction issues, which he may have had even if he'd never been the Shawn Mendes of his time.

The sort of lore that surrounds child actors is that they are doted upon, living a magical life. But the minute the clock strikes midnight and their voice changes and they aren't that cute anymore, their fame disappears and they are back in rags sitting by an ash-filled fireplace. It must be a great shock to go from being "wanted" to "unwanted," particularly as a child.

How does it feel to have peaked in your single-digit years? It makes me wonder: Would I rather have money and fame and lose it all or never have it in the first place?

Michael Jackson said, "I think every child star suffers

through this period because you're not the cute and charming child that you were. You start to grow, and they want to keep you little forever." According to David Hosier, who writes about childhood trauma, the main factors that child celebrities have to deal with are manipulation for financial gain, unwanted pressure, long hours spent working in the limelight, feelings that they are living out someone else's dreams, exposure to drugs and sex, and isolation from "normal" society.

All of these can cause famous children to regress to an even less mature state, suffer from depression, have anxiety attacks, and be extra clingy to their caregivers. As teenagers, they can suffer from drug and alcohol abuse, self-harm, and eating disorders.

Child celebrities can also be easy prey to some of the creeps in the entertainment business, like Jimmy Savile. Savile was a huge TV and radio personality in Britain for more than three decades, including starring in a show called *Jim'll Fix It*. There were rumors while he was alive that he was a child molester, and after he died it was revealed that he'd sexually abused more than five hundred children.

In 2016, former child star Elijah Wood gave an interview to the UK's *Sunday Times* in which he addresses the issue of child sexual abuse in Hollywood: "I never went to parties where that kind of thing was going on. This bizarre industry presents so many paths to temptation. If you don't have some kind of foundation, typically from family, then it will be difficult to deal with." Wood said he had not been a victim of sexual abuse.

However, Corey Feldman, who clearly didn't have a strong family foundation, says he most certainly was abused. "Ask anybody in our group of kids at that time: They were passing us [Feldman and Corey Haim] back and forth to each other," Feldman told the *Hollywood Reporter*. He quotes Alison Arngrim as saying, "'Everybody knew that the two Coreys were just being passed around,'" and adds, "Like it was something people joked about on studio lots." Feldman says he'd been molested and given every single kind of drug.

It is painfully easy to come across stories of child celebrities who have not survived the life. The stresses in such a life are difficult for adults; for children they can be downright impossible to manage.

To be a celebrity means to have more than the usual assault on one's ego," Charles Figley, director of the Traumatology Institute at Tulane University, wrote. "You're very vulnerable to the personal evaluations of other people. The public is ultimately in control of whether your career continues."

To be constantly evaluated like that, to live under that relentless judgment and scrutiny, would be enough to drive you to the kinds of drugs that some people are eager to ply celebrities with.

Given how unusual and stressful the lives of child celebrities are, I understand why some former child stars would want to be around other former child stars: they understand the pitfalls and perils. Just like others who have shared an unusual experience, such as growing up in a commune, child actors can draw some comfort from others who've walked the same path they have.

In the early 1990s, Quinn Cummings left acting and turned away from that kind of celebrity. Thanks to her mother, Quinn had saved enough money to raise her own child with her husband the way she wanted to. She turned her talent and attention to writing and has published three successful books. She's homeschooled her daughter, Anneke, who, in addition to being a stellar kid, has been working on creating a new social network called Xirkl.

If Quinn is an example of a young actress who became famous without trying, Isabel Gillies is at the other end of the spectrum: a talented actress who also started young and for her own reasons never had the ambition to become a celebrity. And she could have.

"At age eighteen I did a movie called *Metropolitan*," she told me. "It turned out to be a big hit. When the director, Whit Stillman, came to my high school drama teacher looking for young women to audition, I was at NYU at that point, but my teacher contacted me. I thought, 'What the heck is a movie with no studio behind it, a porno? You aren't Mike Nichols, and we are shooting in the middle of the *night*? I don't think I'm taking time off college for this!' Also, I got into this great photography class. But the script was beautiful, and Whit convinced me that I would be stupid not to do it. My parents said, 'You're over eighteen—you decide.'"

So Isabel took the part. She went back and forth between college and shooting the movie. *Metropolitan* was released in 1990, its screenplay was nominated for an Oscar, and the movie attracted both an audience and huge media coverage.

But it was a very long time before Isabel worked again as an actress. "The thing about being really famous, like Sharon Stone or Jennifer Lawrence famous, is that I think you *really* have to want it, and I only kind of wanted it," she admitted. "I remember being in Los Angeles for television pilot season in the early 1990s. I was sharing an apartment with the [now famous] actor Alessandro Nivola. We were leaving the apartment, both on our way to auditions. I was wearing some version of what I always wore: ripped jeans, sloppy T-shirt, and no makeup. He was dressed to the nines. He said to me, '*What* are you wearing? Is that what you are wearing to audition for a *pilot*? You'll never get it.' I was all defensive and said, 'What? Yes, I will—it's about my personality; not my looks!' He said, 'You're being stupid. Of course it's about your looks. You have to think about these things. You don't want to blow an audition—ever.' I always blew auditions, and I think it was because I ultimately didn't want the job. I had some ambition, but not a ton, and I think you need a ton."

I understood. Though Isabel is a terrific actress, she would rather be walking her dog than walking down the red carpet at an event. She doesn't have a burning desire to be a celebrity. "If I really wanted to be famous, I wouldn't have had children. In my late twenties, I started getting parts more and more frequently, and suddenly I was kind of in a zone. I was on two TV shows on different networks, and I was doing little movies pretty frequently, *and* I had gotten married. I was working with a wonderful actor who ended up having a huge part on *Lost*. We were talking one day about having kids. He said, 'You can't have kids now! You're killing it. If you have a baby now, you will never be famous. You just won't work enough because—sorry, but you're almost too old!' I was nearing thirty.

"But I said, 'Are you nuts? *Of course* I'm going to have kids. That's not even a question!' So I did, and even though I did end up having a great little part on *Law and Order* that lasted a long time, I didn't become a famous actress. I didn't want it enough."

Isabel Gillies is one of the most down-to-earth, grounded people I know. She (and Caitlin) are invariably the first people I call when I freak out about some aspect of parenting. Even though she looks like a movie star, she doesn't act like one.

"Fame is just . . . strange," she says. "I know a lot of famous people from over the years, and although with most of them if you spend enough time and the right kind of time, the fame disappears, it's always a thing. Usually they are really busy working, so you don't see them. Or it can just be weird because no matter what anyone says, fame separates people. I remember I was friends with this guy for years and years, and then he got really famous and married someone famous. One night I saw him at a restaurant, and even though in the past we were such good friends—he came to parties at my house—that night I looked at him (he was sitting with the entire cast of *Saturday Night Live*) and I didn't say hello. Someone I was with said, 'Aren't you friends with that guy?' And I had been. But something about the fame stopped me from doing the normal thing and saying hi."

For every Isabel and Quinn, there are dozens of Coreys, Dana Platos, and Leif Garretts. Celebrity can add spice to life or swallow you whole. When I came to understand this, I stopped feeling angry that my mother didn't pluck me from my suburban obscurity and whisk me to Broadway auditions or to Los Angeles for TV show auditions (again, shout-out to my lack of talent).

The complicated world of child actors reminded me of Pinocchio on Pleasure Island, but there are no Jiminy Crickets or Blue Fairies to fix their problems. Making it over those endless hurdles without falling seems nothing short of miraculous. But there are people who have done it. And I want to know how.

Intermission 2

It was at a book party about twelve years ago. I had conceived and edited an essay anthology called The Bitch in the House, *so naturally my husband, who's also a writer, followed with his essay anthology* The Bastard on the Couch. *And one of his contributors, Panio Gianopoulos, is married to Molly Ringwald. So Molly came to Dan's book party with Panio.*

I had grown up in the era of The Breakfast Club *and* Sixteen Candles, *so even though by the time of the party Molly wasn't quite as famous anymore, I still thought of her as a Big Star. I can't remember whether I knew she was coming or not, but when I saw her, I thought, "Oh my God!" She was sitting by herself on a couch. She was just sitting there looking bored, or shy, or basically like she wasn't having much fun at all.*

What I should have done was go up to her and say hi. She's a few years younger than me, and I think she might even have just had a baby at that time, so I easily could have asked her about that, or started some sort of conversation . . . I didn't have to shriek, "Oh my GOD, you're Molly Ringwald! Can I please sit near you/breathe your same air?" In other words, I could have treated her like an actual person—one who was nice enough to come to my husband's book party.

Instead, my first thought was that she must be bombarded with starstruck people wherever she goes, and that must be annoying—which I was completely projecting; I mean, maybe she loves that attention! I also didn't want to be some fawning fan. Because the fact that our culture elevates physical beauty, and success in the profession of acting—two things that predictably often go together—to the very, very top of the hierarchy of humankind, over brilliance, originality, creativity, patience, even kindness and generosity, doesn't mean that I do that myself, or that I buy into that silliness. I don't, and I wanted her to know that. Put another way, I didn't want to be a star fucker.

So instead, I ignored her. I avoided talking to her or even making eye contact. Later, of course, I felt like a jerk. Because by refusing to talk to this lonely, bored woman purely because I didn't want to buy into the culture of idealizing and idolizing celebrities, I did exactly that: made her into someone unreal and untouchable, put her on a pedestal she probably didn't even want to be on, and then left her all alone there.

—CATHI HANAUER

★

It was a week after Titanic had opened. I was waiting for a table at Jerry's in New York, standing by the door, possibly for days. It had become hard to gauge the passage of time. I was trying to impress my friend Mitra, who was in town and had complained that she never got to see celebrities. Jerry's was the place to see brunching celebrities.

We'd formed a desperate community in the foyer, our little hopeful bunch. A group of four had just been told they could have the big table in the front window. We looked to them as the alpha group.

Suddenly, the door swung open, and a flood of guys poured through: East Village–looking guys, just rolled out of bed, bleary. We were crushed against the walls. I was lucky to have the sturdy door frame to lean on. The cascade halted and stabilized. One guy was stranded in front of me, dazed. He looked up at me, and his features came together. This was no guy. This was Mr. Titanic himself, the Prince of Dreamy.

He saw the look of recognition on my face, and anxiety— nay, terror—came over his. Was I going to squeal? I smiled instead. He smiled back. He looked like he was twelve. We stood for a moment, a long moment. He knocked his head down and to the side and looked up at me with that Leo look, that puppy-dog, forsake-your-family-and-drink-this-poison look. Then he was swept off again, and immediately seated . . . at the big table in the front window.

The alpha group looked upset. Who were these young turks taking their table? No official explanation had been given. I leaned over and explained snarkily to the group, "It's Leonardo DiCaprio." Instead of sharing my contempt, the alpha group got giddy. "Really?" they stage-whispered, eyes wide. A pre–Spider-Man Tobey Maguire shyly turned around *in his chair to see the girl Leo was talking about. I know I have a certain appeal. You get used to it. I was wearing very flattering lipstick.*

After brunch, as we were walking to the subway, I turned to Mitra and said, "See, I promised you we'd see a celebrity if we ate at Jerry's!" She said, "Why? Who was there?"

—JEN DEADERICK

★

It was 1999. I was twenty-two years old and had recently moved to Los Angeles to make it big as a TV writer. I got a job as an assistant on a CBS show, and while on the lot, I saw a guy with whom I went to high school. What were the odds? Miami Beach was far, far away.

I couldn't remember his name but I knew his face, so I went up to say hi.

"I'm Sascha. I'm pretty sure we went to high school together."

"No. We didn't. I'm Luke Perry."

He was gracious. Said it happens all the time. I was mortified. But considering I hadn't missed a single episode of 90210, in a way I did go to high school with him.

—SASCHA ROTHCHILD

THREE

THE WISDOM OF NOT BELIEVING YOUR OWN HYPE

★

Like Quinn Cummings, Timothy Hutton started acting young. But unlike Quinn, he has continued to work as an actor for more than forty years. And while he's had great fame, he's also worked to keep a semblance of a normal life while dealing with celebrity and all its trappings. Though he has been married to a famous actress (who is the mother of one of his two sons), for the most part he has chosen to live life as a normal guy, albeit one who earned an Academy Award before he hit twenty. He has a unique perspective on celebrity life from the inside.

The first time I saw Timothy Hutton I was thirteen years old and his lovely, pained face filled the screen of the Bedford Hills movie theater. I remember I stopped eating my popcorn when I saw him. That's a kind of love, when you stop eating movie popcorn. He was playing the delicate, damaged Conrad Jarrett in Robert Redford's *Ordinary People*, and he would go on to win an Oscar as best supporting actor for his performance. So I guess I wasn't the only one who fell in love with him then.

That fall I lay on my bed looking at a photo spread of Timothy Hutton in *Seventeen* magazine while listening to Steve Winwood's "While You See a Chance." I haven't seen the magazine in more than thirty years, but I still remember one particular image: Timothy Hutton is on a beach at sunset, his hair longer than it is in the movie, and he is smiling with his whole face—very un-Conrad-like, strong and confident and joyful. I remember staring at the pictures until I felt my heart would burst. Only then did I carefully close the magazine so I could concentrate on homework, every so often sneaking another peek. Finally, when I was sure I could handle it, I cut out all the pictures and taped them to my wall at eye level, alongside some photos of my past true loves. My own Wall of Fame.

I know now it was infinitely safer to love famous movie stars than the boys in my school, with their unretouched faces, saliva-drenched kisses, and grabby hands trying to get under my shirt. My love for movie actors ultimately transferred to a love of movies themselves, which is what I studied in college. (We called them *films*.)

Years passed, and one day as a grown-up I saw Timothy Hutton on Columbus Avenue not far from my apartment. It was 1996. My heart sped up a little, and suddenly I was the thirteen-year-old me again. He was a very nice-looking man and I was by then a cool New Yorker with a boyfriend. I looked at him briefly, as if he'd never been my everything. We passed without acknowledging each other, like the hip, together adults we were—

which made sense, as he had no idea who I was. And that was that.

Cut to late 2009. I had moved from my safe, cozy apartment in a charming neighborhood to a shitty, scary neighborhood and I was feeling somewhat (OK, very) lonely and isolated. I had joined Twitter at some point, but now I was going onto the site more regularly and noticed that people I knew were chatting with the Man Himself, Mr. Timothy Hutton.

I followed him on Twitter and he followed me back and for a moment I had that "I am done" feeling: anything I had ever hoped for had been surpassed in one glaring moment of celebrity virtual connection. It was like the time in high school when the boy I had a crush on gave me a ride in his white Corvette. When I got home, I told my mother I could die now. (She said, "Please don't." Always wise, my mom.)

At the time, Timothy Hutton was between seasons of his show *Leverage*, and he had some spare moments and was exploring social media. We began to chat online and then off. He was a New Yorker, his older son lived in my neighborhood, and soon enough we began to talk the way friends do—that is, friends when one of them has had a mad lifelong crush on the other and the other is a famous movie star who has no idea. You know.

A couple of years later I was moving toward divorce, and he'd been through it twice, both times with children, and he became a good friend to talk to about what to expect. We also discussed books and real estate, and once I even helped him come up with interview questions for Mary Tyler Moore for a piece he was writing for *TV Guide*. (The "I can die nows" were coming fast and furious.)

Later he gamely appeared in a short movie I put together for one of my books. Sometime after that we had breakfast and we talked about writing projects, but mostly our relationship was about me saying over and over inside my head, "OHMYGOD OHMYGOD, IT'S TIMOTHY HUTTON/CONRAD JAR-RETT!"

I have to admit that every time I talked to, texted with, or met Tim, I felt like Mia Farrow's character must have felt in *The Purple Rose of Cairo*. I knew Tim first as a movie star at the time of my life when I was most likely to fall in love with a fictional character. As Mia's character, Cecilia, says in the movie, "I just met a wonderful man. He's fictional, but you can't have everything." How right she is.

In person, Timothy Hutton looks pretty much as he does on-screen. Unlike most stars you meet, he is tall (for a human, not just an actor). And he doesn't have any weird dyed hair or Botox. He is—and this is a huge compliment—"normal." Because of this, it was odd to talk to him about celebrity. To his credit, he was gracious. He was working in Los Angeles when I wanted to interview him, but he made time for me when I traveled there to interview other people.

Now, I am a New Yorker. I don't own a car, and I don't think about car things. I rented a small green four-wheeler, and while driving to Tim's rented house at the appointed time, I realized that I did not bring a car charger for my iPhone, and I was using it as a GPS, so suddenly I realized I was running down my phone's battery. (Outlets are the public bathrooms of the 2000s, but that's the subject of another book.) This sort of secondary worry would not have been so dramatic to me if I was visiting a non-celebrity friend. I really didn't want to ask him to plug in my phone. The shame! The inconvenience! The fear he had a flip phone!

This sounds ridiculous, I know. Tim is such a gracious person that when he noticed that I had brought my own (used) plastic water bottle, he took it away and gave me a blue glass bottle of Saratoga water because it matched my outfit better. No, just kidding. He said the plastic bottles give you cancer.

When I first arrived at Tim's house, I had to change from sneakers, which I drive in, to grown-up casual sandals. It took me so long to do this (for reasons I won't get into) that Tim actually came out of his house and stood by my rental car, waiting for me. I think he was worried I'd forgotten how to open the car door. As I struggled into my sandals, I kept thinking of the glamorous, sophisticated, world-weary entrance I'd imagined I was going to make. But given how inept my arrival was and that he was Timothy Hutton and that I had sock imprints on my feet, I ditched all my funny opening lines because I realized this was an awkward start and moved on. To another awkward start.

So far he and I had always talked as if he was a regular guy who hadn't been on the cover of a tabloid when his marriage broke up. So when the two of us sat down to talk, I tried to transition into the reason I was there. But it was odd: it wasn't like when I was a writer who had been hired by magazines to interview people. Again, as I had felt with Quinn Cummings, I cared whether Timothy Hutton liked me. Maybe knowing a celebrity even slightly does that.

We began by talking about our children and school. I asked if his fame had caused him to experience any weirdness among parents.

"Oh, you know, sometimes you're standing on the sidelines of your kid's game talking to another parent, and it would be a very normal conversation. And then there would be a pause, and I could feel it coming. It might be something general like, 'What's it like?' And that would hang in the air. If I was in a particularly generous mood, I would finish the sentence for them and say it's like any other job and say, 'You know, work is work.' You certainly can't approach it like you're doing something special and amazing. Then I would say after that I am very fortunate to work in the field because it's fun and it pays well and things like that. There are things you can say and you know you're giving them material for their next cocktail party."

What, I asked, does he say if he's not feeling very generous?

"Well, then they would say, 'What's it like?' and I would ask, 'What's what like?' Then they would say, 'You know—what you do.' I would still say, 'I'm not sure I'm following.' And they'd say, 'You know what I'm talking about,' and I would say, 'No, I don't.' Which wasn't true, but it was more entertaining to me, because I knew at some point I would have to address it but at least with the opening exchange I would set the ground rules. If you want to do this, don't be cute about it: ask and let's get this over with.

"Or someone comes up to you and says, 'I loved you in *Shawshank Redemption*.' You can either say 'thank you' and leave it at that. Or you can say, 'You're thinking of Tim Robbins. I'm Tim Hutton.' That's probably the best way to handle it. After a bunch of these encounters you realize they'll argue with you.

Or they'll say, 'What was that movie you were in where you play the astronaut?' And you say, 'I was never in a movie where I play an astronaut.' And then they'll say, 'Yes, you were' and turn to their wife for confirmation. It kind of gets crazy how this conversation goes."

The ease with which people recognize that someone is famous but forget the reason someone is famous must be annoying.

"It's easy for people to come away thinking you're a jerk," Tim admitted.

There's a phenomenon in New York (and maybe other cities) where people are paid to stand on the sidewalks and as you walk by ask, "Are you interested in supporting gay rights?" They are paid to solicit money and you learn not to make eye contact or you pretend you're on the phone. I imagine that being a celebrity out in the world is a lot like that, and I asked Tim if that's about right.

"Yeah," Tim agreed. "I don't know what I would do if everyone recognized me whenever I walk into the room, like Tom Cruise. I was in a play once in New York and Tom Cruise was in the audience and we knew it halfway through the performance because you can see and feel that half the audience has turned around and is looking at him. It was amazing because when those of us in the play left the theater, he couldn't even get backstage to say hi because there were hundreds of people who had heard Tom Cruise was at this play.

"My son, Noah, is twenty-eight now, so he's older. But I've had experiences with him over the years, and his mom is also a recognized actor [Debra Winger]. I remember being around

New York or traveling with him and strangers would come up to us. I knew it wasn't reasonable to assume it would never happen, especially going to the airport or walking in New York, unless you wore a ridiculous disguise. And it never really happened to me that much anyway. But the place where you can feel kind of ambushed is in a restaurant. People can say, 'Well, you're out at a restaurant. You can eat at home.' My response is always, 'Why can't I go out to a restaurant?' Most people won't approach the table, but some people do and they approach it when it's just you and your ten-year-old kid and you're deep in conversation and you're talking to him and having a meal. And someone comes up and says, 'Hey,' and interrupts and wants to engage. If they wanted a photo, I'd say, 'I'm having dinner with my son right now. Do you mind if we do it after?' Most people would look at me and get offended and upset about that. A lot would not bother to come back, and I would make the dinner last longer and wait them out. I just thought it was weird for my son. Some people would just come and sit down and start talking to me. I've never, ever lost it and told them to leave or that they're rude, because I learned a long, long time ago that if you give people that story, they'll tell it ten times more than the story when you're just being nice. It multiplies like crazy if you're not nice to them."

Yes, I know, because one of my most told stories is about when I was in college in New York City. I worked at the Banana Republic store at 87th Street and Broadway. It was my first day on the cash register, which was significant for two reasons: The first is I'm dreadful at math and the opposite of exacting (let's call it "careless"). Also, if I make one mistake, it somehow breeds more. I'm like Rosalind Russell in *Auntie Mame* who takes a job at Macy's during the Christmas rush.

My first customer was a nice Hasidic guy who was buying a lot of clothes for his kids. When I screwed up ringing up his purchases, he patiently let me start over and helped me get the transaction right.

The next customer was not so gracious.

When I screwed up, he got really mad, and when I started over, I was worried I was missing something and he said, "Oh, for God sakes! Get someone who can do this!"

I know, many people would react this way. But you should be a little more careful if you're ROBERT DUVALL.

Tim nodded and said, "It's hard, because even me saying 'now isn't a good time' can turn into 'what a prick that guy was.' Politeness for you turns out to be impoliteness to them. So it's good to be polite or manage the moment—to make them feel like they had a moment." Someone should tell that to Mr. Duvall.

Of course Timothy Hutton has another perspective on this as well. He was also the son of a famous actor, Jim Hutton, who was in films like *Where the Boys Are* and the hit TV series *Ellery Queen*. I wonder if Tim's experience as the child of a celebrity informed his choices with his own kids.

"Oh sure," he said. "I remember being out to dinner with my father, and people would come up to the table and compliment him, and at some point their attention shifted over to me." He continued, "I remember feeling extremely uncomfortable and also upset that my time with my dad was being cut into like this. And the attention on me was totally unearned. I think people just wanted to prolong the interaction." He added, "They were nice people and it wasn't their fault. It's just how it felt to me."

L ike everything in life, there is a right way to engage a celebrity. And there's a right way for a celebrity to engage with the public.

"I think you should be nice to people in public—not just because you want them to see your movies, but because it's a nice way to go about life," Tim explained. "You should always be polite. But if people get out of line, you should recalibrate them so they do get up from the table but they walk away thinking they had a pleasant experience or that they apologize, to which you respond, 'Oh, no, it's completely OK.'"

We were sitting in the kitchen of Tim's rental house when the door to the backyard opened and an electronic voice from the security system said, "Someone is entering the kitchen." It was a friend of Tim's, a movie producer named Charlie, who was staying in Tim's guesthouse. He apologized for interrupting, and Tim and I both said—in the argot I just learned—that it's completely OK. While Charlie made himself a bagel, Tim told him who I was and described the book trailer we'd made. We showed it to him and he laughed. Tim said, "There wasn't a script or anything. We just did it."

(This is true. When I asked Tim to be in it and he agreed, there was a big part of me that didn't believe it would actually happen. I had a suspicion that I'd show up on the day we were to shoot it at the office of my publisher, the other actor in the video, and we'd wait and wait for Tim to show up, and he never would, and then I'd go home feeling disappointed. But on the subway ride to the shoot, I realized Timothy Hutton might actually show up, so I needed to be prepared. I wrote a bunch of notes for what I wanted him to say on the back of a receipt. My idea was to use his literary interests as a jumping-off point for the video. I would suggest on camera to my publisher that instead of putting together a silly book trailer, Tim and I would have a literary discourse that would be filmed, then Tim would enter, and he and I would start talking, and it would turn out that he was really stupid. We shot a version of that and it didn't work. So Tim switched his "character" to being an asshole movie star, and it turned out really well.)

Tim's friend Charlie turned out to be Charles Wessler, who produced several Farrelly brothers movies and is best friends with Carrie Fisher and Griffin Dunne. He and Tim told me the story of how they once gave a party and put the stuffed dog from *There's Something about Mary* in the freezer and then would ask girls to get them some ice and watch their reactions when they opened the freezer. They laughed very hard, while also admitting it wasn't very nice of them. Charlie disappeared out the door, and Tim and I continued to dissect the meaning of celebrity.

What I really wanted to know from Tim was what he was doing when I was infatuated with him after *Ordinary People*. When I was lying on my bed, looking at his picture in *Seventeen* magazine, holding it so close to my face that our eyes were locked, thinking about running down the beach with him in a white bikini and someone else's body, what was he doing? I was pretty sure he wasn't thinking about me.

When I asked Tim, he tilted his head and said politely, "You do know that I didn't know you existed then, right?"

Sadly, yes. But I beckoned him to go on anyway. It took him a minute to go back there, and it was terribly exciting for me. When someone famous thinks about a time when you are thinking about them, it's like you have a glimpse into another dimension—a Vulcan mind meld with a window into a world where everybody knows you or wants to know about you.

"It's an interesting thing when you look back on a period of time," he said. "It seems like it happened quickly. You know people say, 'All of the sudden . . .' But it's not like that. It's gradual. By the time you'd seen *Ordinary People*, I had read for the part seven times, found out I got the role, filmed it, then it was edited for a year—I was doing a play at one point. Then I went on a publicity tour for the movie and talked to critics who hadn't actually even seen the film, just some clips . . . It wasn't 'all of the sudden' for me. I think the assumption is that *Ordinary People* came out and there was this radical change. You know, the next day I was living in a mansion with twenty sports cars and cooks and maids."

I understood that—as adult Julie. But the other one, the thirteen-year-old Julie, still thought he *was* Conrad Jarrett.

"Things did change . . . slowly. The project after that, I got paid more. Also I was hired to be a supporting role in *Taps*, and two weeks after *Ordinary People* came out, the producer called and offered me the lead." He was looking out the window as memories came back to him. "I do remember being on some talk show, and it was at Rockefeller Center and I was in this car, and we pulled up to those huge revolving doors. I'm sort of casually walking and I look off to the side and think, 'Hmm, there's a lot of young girls hanging out there.' And one of them turns and sees me and in slow motion mouths, 'THERE HE IS!' They were hanging out to see me. I didn't put it together at all.

"I guess after *Taps* my life did change in that I bought a car and a house and there were no more auditions. Mostly the people in my life stayed the same. I had this tight group of actor friends and one of them kept saying to me, 'Don't let this change you! Don't let this change you!' He kept saying it over and over, and I finally said, 'You know, that goes for you as well.' And I didn't see him much after that."

In the same way I feel funny about asking him to plug in my phone, I understand that people change around celebrities. I worked for David Letterman for about a year, and almost the whole time I felt excited that he was *David Letterman*. I remember interviewing Parker Posey for a magazine piece several years ago, and we were walking down the street she lived on in Greenwich Village, and I loved that people looked at me and saw that I was with her, like I must be special. Or when I'm with my friend Ann, who is one of my closest friends in the world, I still act goofy around her celebrity husband.

Tim has experienced something similar. "I remember I had an uncle who really had nothing to do with us. He didn't give a shit about my sister and me and then suddenly [after *Ordinary People*] he gets in touch with my mother. He asked would I like to invest in this company he's working for, and I told him send me the information. I read it and told him it wasn't something I was interested in. That was thirty years ago and I never heard from him again. A lot of people have this misplaced idea of my 'wealth.'"

When you're a celebrity, people have a tendency to believe you're rich, which isn't always the case. Dolly Parton talks about people who are "hick rich," which is when people who aren't rich to begin with start making money and use it to buy expensive things they don't need and go through their money quickly. You may remember MC Hammer appearing on VH1 after losing his thirty million dollars. But if you Google any celebrity, a page will come up with their "net worth." Every celebrity I've showed this to has laughed.

Tim doesn't talk about money and I don't ask, but clearly he is doing fine and he manages it quite sanely. This may be because although he got famous early in his career—not as a child star but as a young adult new on the scene—and won awards for his early work, he matured into his fame. You could say he kind of broke in his celebrity, as you might a (beguiling) leather chair that gets more comfortable to sit in over time.

"It's never been a burden to me," Tim said. "It's just been this odd thing that's happened to me ever since the first movie came out a long time ago. You try to handle it well. I understand why some people haven't handled it well. There are people who couldn't go out without photographers sitting outside their apartment, and TMZ is there trying to piss them off with obnoxious questions, and they can't eat outside. I don't know how I would handle that. There really are people who can't go anywhere without it being a big occurrence."

. . .

For Timothy Hutton, who confronted fame so early, being a celebrity has always been part of being an actor. It was more of a job than it was for some of the people who became a success later. It's clear that Tim wanted to be an actor more than he wanted to be famous. While he certainly is a successful actor, he works hard and has to keep working.

"There are people who think I can call up and just be in the next *Avengers*," Tim said ruefully. Which of course I think is horrible: of course Timothy Hutton should be in any movie he wants to be in!

But the more I think about it, the more I realize that there is a difference between celebrity and success. And having one doesn't necessarily mean that you have the other.

Intermission 3

A few years ago, I was hurrying through Rockefeller Center, late for an appointment with my dentist. My head was down and I was talking to myself, so I'm sure I looked deranged. I collided, hard, with a man, and looked up, irritated, into the intense blue eyes of—oh, my—Viggo Mortensen.

He was trailed by twitchy handlers who were escorting him to some talk show. He had on a light blue shirt, some sort of hip navy jacket, and jeans. He didn't speak. For three of the most erotic seconds of my life, I transformed into

Arwen in Lord of the Rings, *standing at the altar as she marries Aragorn.*

It was so satisfying because he looked the way you hoped he would look: he wasn't short like so many celebrities. He didn't have a large head, he wasn't lacquered with product. He was tall and had broad shoulders and beautiful wavy hair. He looked like he could build things out of wood.

—JANCEE DUNN

Right after I gave birth to my son—like, the day afterward—shooting began on the film adaptation of my novel Animal Husbandry. *I'd gained about seventy pounds during my pregnancy and was waddling around in postnatal elastic pants when I started getting emails and phone calls from the producer, Lynda Obst (1), telling me that the director Tony Goldwyn (2) and stars Ashley Judd (3), Hugh Jackman (4), Greg Kinnear (5), Marisa Tomei (6), and Ellen Barkin (7) were hoping I would come to New York so that I could be in a big party scene they were planning to shoot. Be in a big party scene?! This fat?! I don't think so! But I did agree to drive in from Washington, DC, where we were living at the time, to visit the set. It was August, hot and humid, and it was not an easy drive: My husband's mother and his daughter from a previous marriage as well as our six-week-old were in the backseat, and there had already been some yelling about turning off the Harry Potter audiobooks cassette tapes that had played endlessly on the trip. And then came an insane accusation from my husband, who was driving, that I* was "withholding directions" to TriBeCa (the one area in New York where neither of us had lived when we'd both lived in New York). But finally we got there, sweaty and angry, wild-eyed and frizzy-haired, and almost instantly Hugh Jackman, who had just adopted a little boy named Oscar, bent down to look at my son in his portable car seat and started talking to us about diaper changing and sleeping and feeding schedules. There's a picture somewhere to prove this happened and that I'm not making it up.

—LAURA ZIGMAN

★

I was a naïve, young, and eager production coordinator on a TV special celebrating Carnegie Hall's hundredth anniversary in New York City. We were close to showtime and I was riding up to the stage in a huge industrial elevator—the kind with gates that rise up and pull down, meeting in the middle, and that travels very slowly and deliberately. You could probably fit a car in this thing. The elevator stopped and two men in tuxedos got on. They didn't speak or even look at me.

Standing across from them, I was in the midst of getting instructions through my walkie-talkie headset. They couldn't hear anything. Just the elevator moving in silence.

Once the transmission ended, I responded to my supervisor, breaking the silence of the elevator, "COPY THAT. I WILL MAKE SURE. I'M HEADING TO THE STAGE NOW."

One of the men looked up at me, trying to contain his sudden and very real anger, and said, "WILL YOU PLEASE

SHUT UP. THERE MUST BE SILENCE WHEN THE MAESTRO IS PRESENT." *I'm sure I turned a deep shade of red. As I started to apologize, he "SHHHHSHD" me very rigidly with his finger to his mouth. We continued traveling up for what seemed like an eternity; all the while I was getting called on the walkie-talkie and being asked to respond.*

As we arrived to the stage floor, the gate opened and the tuxedoed men walked away. Assuming the men were far enough away from me, I quickly keyed my walkie-talkie to respond to the repeated attempts to contact me. "The Maestro is walking to the stage. I repeat . . ." The man ahead of me—now fully enraged—turned back, "DO NOT REPEAT ANYTHING! THERE MUST BE SILENCE WHEN THE MAESTRO IS PRESENT!"

The show started twenty minutes late. The Maestro was world-renowned conductor James Levine. And he never spoke or looked at me.

—JEFF FISHER

FOUR

THE GAME PLAN FOR CREATING A STAR

★

My father used to say if he hadn't had to worry about supporting a family, he would've gone into radio: He always wanted to be an announcer. He has one of those 1940s radio voices and he's always enjoyed entertaining (he even did a stand-up routine at my wedding, but I'm pretty sure that's not why I got divorced). I think my brothers might have wanted to be professional athletes: Brian maybe a baseball player (Johnny Bench) and Matthew a tennis ace (Arthur Ashe). I wanted to be a Movie Star. Not an actress, a Movie Star. I wanted to walk the red carpet in free fabulous Calvin Klein gowns and fantastic jewels on loan from Harry Winston; I wanted mountains of money and multiple residences; I wanted strangers to adore me from a respectable distance. (I know this isn't how celebrity works. I know about the work and the pain, but neither of those are in my dream.)

I'm aware celebrity is likely not going to happen for me, but it does happen to some people. After watching the 2013 Academy Awards and seeing Christoph Waltz win his second Best Supporting Actor award in three years, I was curious to know how he rose to this spot. While he's nice-enough looking and a great actor, I had never heard of him until he was fifty-two years old—not exactly a young turk. I decided to talk to his agent and see (a) how he helped to make Christoph Waltz a star and (b) whether he could he do it for me. After all, I was only forty-six, practically an ingénue.

Adam Schweitzer is one of the top film agents in the business, and one of the few who is located in New York, at ICM Partners. When I met him, he reminded me of me, if I were a man, and had money, and a driving ambition. In other words, he was a Jew who liked movies.

"I grew up in New York," Adam told me. "When I was a kid, my grandparents were really into show business. They would take me to Broadway shows and old movies, and that was my introduction. For me it was something about actors and watching their performance. I'm a big sports guy, too. I like watching the physical performance and the reaction you get from watching that performance. When I went to college and started taking film classes and theory and understanding how to watch movies in a different way, I started to appreciate it more through a director's eye. I didn't want to be an actor, but I wanted to be involved with actors and help them shape their careers."

His first job was in film production. "I worked for a little production company and spent a lot of my day in an editing room and renting equipment and doing all this stuff I wasn't really interested in. The fact that I got to see things from start to finish was good and would be helpful to me later. There was a guy who ran the company who was almost like an agent—he had all these relationships and was building up talent, and it was fascinating. So I went to him and told him I wanted to shadow him and do what he does. He said there was only one of him there, but that I would make a good agent. I ultimately got my résumé from one person to the next and got an interview at ICM and started as an assistant."

I tell Adam about how when *I* was an agent's assistant, we didn't have computers—we had typewriters. The agent I worked for never allowed a document to go out with Wite-Out on it, so if I made a mistake typing a letter, I would have to start all over again. (NB: I lasted less than three months.)

He remembers the time: "When I started at ICM, there was a guy named Sam Cohn, who was like the biggest agent of his era. I worked for another agent who was kind of a right-hand man to Sam, and I would sit outside his office and be in awe of what Sam did. This was someone who was incredibly cultured and smart. Whether it was a movie or the ballet or opera, he was out to something all the time. He stuck with the art of it—that's what he believed in. And when you look at the people he represented [according to Sam Cohn's *New York Times* obit: Paul Newman, Meryl Streep, Mike Nichols, Nora Ephron, Louis Malle, Arthur Miller, E. L. Doctorow], it was just incredible. He had just a classic business and client list, and for me it was something to aspire to."

When I ask about Christoph Waltz, Adam's eyes light up. "That was a unique situation. That was just reading the script of *Inglourious Basterds,* which was incredible. That role just exploded off the page. It was one of the best parts I had read in a very long time. It was very obvious to me it was a great opportunity for an actor. The producers were deep into casting and they were trying to figure out who would play that part. There was talk that Quentin Tarantino had created an uncastable role, because you had to speak all these languages, and not only did you have to speak them, you had to act in them. The great thing about this part was that it was the ultimate showcase for an actor. This actor needed to be smart and scary and funny and charming and he's acting in four languages. I had become obsessed with seeing who would get this part, so when I realized it wouldn't be someone we represented, I wanted to find the person to represent. I wanted to sign whoever got it, because I knew that person would get the Oscar."

After Waltz was cast, Adam nabbed him. And he was right. Not only did Waltz win an Academy Award for the role, but he also won the Oscar two years later for his performance in *Django Unchained,* which Tarantino also wrote and directed. When Adam Schweitzer is right, he is really right.

In other areas the star makers come with different skill sets. For a time in the late 1990s, Lou Pearlman was the Man when it came to the creating the boy bands of that era.

Pearlman died in federal prison in 2016. Back then he was both a well-known record producer and a manager with an exceptional eye for talent. He also happened to be a dishonest businessman and a sexual predator. But in 1992 he placed an ad in the *Orlando Sentinel* looking for young singers to start a band, bringing the young men together to create the Backstreet Boys, then NSYNC, O-Town, and others. He had a talent for putting together the right combination of voices and faces that would make tens of millions of girls all over the world swoon and use their piggy bank money to buy the bands' CDs and endless array of merchandise. Pearlman, who was known as Big Poppa, was profiled on *60 Minutes II* and *20/20* and also produced the hit ABC/MTV series *Making the Band*. He had a lot of people buying what he was selling. The whole time, though, he was allegedly having inappropriate contact with scores of the young boys he was "mentoring." In an interview in *Vanity Fair*, Rich Cronin, the lead singer of the Pearlman boy band Lyte Funky Ones (LFO), said, "Honestly, I don't think Lou ever thought we would become stars. I just think he wanted cute guys around him; this was all an excuse. And then lightning crazily struck and an empire was created." Only when it was discovered that Pearlman had both stolen money owed to the band members and defrauded investors through a Ponzi scheme did people sue him. The whole messing around with underage boys in exchange for a chance at the big time was an afterthought. Eventually the Backstreet Boys and NSYNC settled their lawsuits. In a 2006 *Rolling Stone* article, Justin Timberlake said he felt like he "was being monetarily raped by a Svengali." Pearlman died in prison in 2016. Timberlake tweeted, "I hope he found some peace. God bless and RIP, Lou Pearlman." While Aaron Carter tweeted, "#LouPearlman my old manager died in prison . . . Rip Lou not the best business guy really at all but he did discover me karma is real."

. . .

As horrible as these stories are, they don't stop throngs of people from doing anything to be discovered and singled out for celebrity. It's the ultimate Cinderella story. We all love it when we hear about a grocery bagger being plucked from obscurity to sing on television and dazzle millions. Or better yet, when the middle-age, frumpily dressed Scot Susan Boyle stood onstage in 2009 in front of Simon Cowell on *Britain's Got Talent* and belted out "I Dreamed a Dream" from *Les Misérables*, gobsmacking the judges and the audience, becoming a YouTube sensation, and then skyrocketing to fame. Her debut album, *I Dreamed a Dream*, became the UK's best-selling debut album of all time. She made everyone feel like anything was possible. Even me.

I ask Adam Schweitzer if he could make me a star, too.

He is a very polite man, but he loses his composure for a second.

"What are you talking about?" he demands.

"I imagine you can pick up the phone and tell Steven Spielberg that you have this woman in your office that he needs to create a vehicle for."

He starts playing with things on his desk.

"I couldn't do that for anyone. Of course I could pick up the phone and get you an audition, but this business is about trust and relationships."

I think what he means is that sending me in for a big audition might not be great for his reputation. (But in fairness to me, he hasn't seen me perform the role of Woman Whose Credit

Card Was Declined at Walgreens. The role was called "a triumph!" by the man standing behind me who was returning a vaporizer.)

He's not convinced, and we move on.

"I have seen people and been blown away—you get a feeling, a physical reaction to their performance. It doesn't happen often, but it has happened."

I find it exhilarating to see someone whose clients become celebrities on the basis of their unique talent. This isn't about a pretty face or the numbers of followers. It's an old-fashioned craft.

When I left his office, I texted my brothers to find out if in fact I was right, that they'd choose to be Ashe and Bench. Nope. Matt said he would want to be Whitney Houston and Brian said Amy Winehouse. Two dead divas. Go figure.

Intermission 4

I had done a few things with Ringo Starr over the past few days because my husband's aunt and uncle are friends with him. We went to a dinner where he sent his food back a couple of times, we went to a concert where afterwards Ringo said, "I just don't get what the deal was about her." He's just a regular guy and I am just here with this regular guy. My husband had come up from Boulder and there was a party and there I was hanging out with my new best friend, Ringo, when he walked up. Ringo and I were chatting, and I was acting like it was really not a big deal. So when my husband—who had not yet officially met Ringo—came over, I said, "This is my husband, Danny." And as they reached out hands to shake, I said, "And, Danny, this is . . ."—long pause that got longer—"this is . . ."

Their hands were done shaking and I was just staring. It wasn't that I couldn't think of his name. It was that all his close friends and family called him Richard. I didn't know if we had reached this phase of our relationship—was I to say "this is Ringo" or "this is Richard"? So I froze. He seemed disappointed. My dreams of becoming super close to him and his wife and kids started to disappear. He had even laughed at a few of my jokes. All that we had built . . . vanished.

My husband tried to save it by saying, "Yeah, I know who this is. I have heard of him. It's Ringo."

And I said, "Yeah, it's Ringo."

Ringo seemed hurt and kind of acted aloof again. He slowly walked away to find someone, someone who called him Richard.

—MAE MARTIN

★

My husband is one of the biggest Beatles fans in the world. He is also one of the few Beatles fans who does not blame Yoko for their demise. He adores her. So, in 1994, when Yoko produced a show that was a thinly veiled account of her time with John Lennon entitled New York Rock, *we were among the first to get tickets. After the show, we waited by the stage door for Yoko to autograph my husband's program. We waited with others, who were cordially and pleasantly greeted by her. Everyone mustered up some kind words, and she responded with very polite "thank yous," and she graciously signed each person's program, one by one. When it came time for my husband, he said something like, "Wonderful show!" and she looked him in the face like he was some kind of escaped convict, ripped the program out of his hand, quickly scribbled her name, and literally threw it back at him, nearly hitting him right between the eyes with it. She then turned on her heels and stormed back inside.*

—LYDIA BUTLER

★

Chris Guest, Michael McKean, and I once were rehearsing for a Spinal Tap music tour, and a guy from the neighboring studio poked his head in. It was Paul McCartney. I was starstruck.

—HARRY SHEARER

FIVE

THE FLAME OF CELEBRITY: DON'T GET TOO CLOSE

★

I first had the idea to talk to Griffin Dunne about celebrity when I read *The Way We Lived Then: Recollections of a Well-Known Name Dropper* by his father, the late Dominick Dunne. I stumbled on the book in a lovely out-of-print book-shop in Le Marais (all right, I got it on eBay), and the whole time I was reading the book—which is mostly wonderful black-and-white photos of Dominick; his former wife, Ellen; and pretty much every famous person of the 1950s and '60s, from actors to singers to politicians—I kept thinking, "I wish I could talk to Dominick Dunne; this is a man who totally understands and loves the phenomenon of celebrity." The parties the Dunnes threw in Hollywood seemed to be the real-life goings-on of what Lucy Ricardo experienced at the Brown Derby, when she, Ricky, and the Mertzes went to Hollywood in *I Love Lucy*. Griffin and his sister, the actress Dominique Dunne, and his brother, Alex, were usually shuffled off to hotels in their pajamas on these occasions, when there was so much glamour in their house that you'd have to shield your eyes.

Aside from having given these fantastic parties, Dominick Dunne was a marvelous storyteller. I had heard him on the radio and watched him on TV, and he was invariably smart, funny, and engaging, and he lived in the thick of celebrity for a large portion of his adult life.

I had interviewed Griffin very briefly in 1995, when I was a stringer for *Premiere* magazine. I had to "cover" the cast party for the movie *Search and Destroy*, which was directed by the artist David Salle and starred Illeana Douglas, Rosanna Arquette, Ethan Hawke, Dennis Hopper, John Turturro, Martin Scorsese, Christopher Walken, and Griffin. My assignment was to get a quote from Walken, but he wouldn't talk to me, and he wasn't nice about it, either, even when I mentioned that I was his next-door neighbor on the Upper West Side and he'd run up and hugged me once because from behind he thought I was his wife. Jerk.

Being the hard-boiled journalist that I was, I said screw it when Walken wouldn't talk to me. I figured I'd stick some hors d'oeuvres in my pocket and get out of there. But a desperate publicist pulled me aside and said she thought she could get Griffin Dunne to chat with me. I was nervous, because though I wasn't an admirer of Walken, I was a huge fan of Griffin Dunne, and if he was mean to me, I don't think I could've taken it.

I had first developed an appreciation for him when I was in high school. I used to watch movies I loved over and over—

hundreds of times (obviously one of the many fantastic benefits of having a moribund social life). One of the movies I loved to rewatch was *An American Werewolf in London,* and I used to do a heralded (at least by my friend Barbara) impression of Griffin as the decaying Jack Goodman. I'd hold a little bit of luncheon meat on my cheek and say, "The undead surround me. Have you ever talked to a corpse? It's boring! I'm lonely! Kill yourself, David, before you kill others!" It was really remarkable, second only to my Shirley Partridge impression.

I need not have worried. When Griffin was introduced to me, he was kind and charming and incredibly smart, and over the years I learned from everyone who knew him that he was an exception to all the famous-actor stereotypes. And so I contacted him again about this book.

Griffin Dunne did not become an actor to be famous. He didn't want to be a celebrity. Though he grew up in Hollywood with parents who gave huge parties filled with the names and faces from the billboards lining Sunset Boulevard and spilling out of newspaper and magazine headlines, he wanted to be a lowercase-*a* actor. In the eulogy he gave at his father's funeral, Griffin likened himself to the narrator of the Simon and Garfunkel song "The Boxer": gritty, struggling, urban, with just a pocketful of mumbles.

"I was telling this guy who had just got into NYU about my experiences as an actor," Griffin says. We are talking at a café, the kind that people often have interviews in, in an area of downtown New York City that I've never been to, though I've lived in the city for close to thirty years. "I said there's a statistic where any acting class you're in, after five years, only half of the people currently in the room will be in the business, and then ten years after that, only eight percent will still be in the business, and then anytime after that, maybe one or two percent will still be in the business. The guy finished my sentence for me: 'That's the same fucking thing you hear in every acting class.' It's like the general giving his troops the 'you might not come back' speech, but it's incredibly true."

What's fascinated me about Griffin is his seeming ambivalence about celebrity; yet it was his choice to become an actor, and in order to be successful you must contend with celebrity. Unless, that is, you flatly don't want that and refuse to be cast in anything more visible than your community theater's presentation of *Inherit the Wind*. And this isn't true just for actors. Professional athletes are great talents before they sign huge endorsement deals. The same is true for famous politicians before they leave office and become lobbyists or consultants. Fame isn't always the goal, nor is it always the ultimate sign of success. Many great athletes and political figures are far from being household names and have had their success without the glare of celebrity shining down on them.

But acting is different. It is performing. And if you do it well and consistently and have a bit of luck, people will start to recognize you. You'll get famous. And depending on what kind of fame it is, that could be a problem.

I explain this thought to Griffin, who nods as I speak.

"When I was growing up in that environment . . . I was just so young that I would love to know then what I know now. I would have loved to have sat on a couch and talked to Billy Wilder and William Wyler and David Niven and all these incredibly legendary people." In that moment he looks like he's seeing a memory that I so badly wish I could watch with him.

"I look at those pictures [like a photo of him in his father's book] and I was only eight years old. The only one who I *knew* was INCREDIBLY famous was Sean Connery, who was in our pool during the time of *From Russia with Love.*

"It had just come out and I had seen it just like any other kid, and he was bald, which I noticed when I saw him in person. So before I knew what a toupee was, I knew what a toupee was. I must have been five or six, because I didn't really know how to swim. I was so deranged by this famous person being in my pool that I jumped in the pool to show him I could swim. He must have realized what was up from dealing with so many fans and girls and he didn't freak out about it. When I jumped in and sunk to the bottom of the pool, he, without a sound, swooped down and grabbed me by my trunks and pulled me out and put me by the side of the pool and said"—here Griffin does a phenomenal Sean Connery brogue— "'Maybe it's a little bit too soon for that, laddie.'"

We sit for a moment and reflect on that. Then I tell Griffin about the time in 1978 when my brothers and cousins and I spotted film critic Gene Shalit on East 58th Street and Third Avenue. We saw him go into a restaurant and we raced to a stationery store and bought a pad and pencil (the pads they had were about two inches square and the pencil was the size of a tiny sewing needle). We waited outside the restaurant for at least an hour for him to come out and had him sign an autograph for each of us. All that would fit on the pad was "Gene Shalit" in script. We then went back to the stationery store and bought tiny gold frames for our treasures. So I knew how he felt about Sean Connery in his pool.

"Yes!" Griffin says. "That was exactly like it!" And my love for him deepens.

Other than Sean Connery, Griffin didn't know a lot about who was wandering around his house at the time. "Not to get too Freudian on it, but with the dinner guests and the parties and black tie and the orchestras and the takeout chili from Chasen's that would be served at two thirty or three in the morning—that was the priority for my dad. We were in our pajamas when they were doing these things and doing our homework in hotel rooms, so we weren't at the parties. I was growing up with more of a resentment toward Hollywood and fame than any kind of attraction for it. It took my parents' attention from me. I wanted to leave Los Angeles for as long as I could remember. As soon as I could, I went to New York, because I knew that New York didn't give a shit about that. When I was eighteen, I moved here. I had an impatience and almost disgust with people who were feverish about fame that it was almost nauseating to look at. My favorite book was in fact *The Day of the Locust*, when all those people tore that guy to pieces on the street. That was actually one of the earliest books I ever read and that made an enormous impact on me . . . That was the Hollywood I recognized.

"I resented the celebrity world, but at the same time I realized after being in New York and wanting to be an actor, I was just doing theater and off-off-off-off-off Broadway—there couldn't be enough *offs* for what I considered legitimate and deserved my presence.

"Fame and celebrity were revered at both the dinner table and the dinner parties my parents gave, as it was and will always be in Hollywood. I never didn't want to be an actor; I just didn't want to make my bones in LA. I earnestly believed New York was a place where talent trumped fame, where the work 'speaks for itself' and self-promotion was a cardinal sin. New York actors, I believed, would rather work on the stage and turn down the Oscar no matter how many times they won. At the age of eighteen, I couldn't wait to move to New York to turn down an Academy Award. Now it's different. Dylan and De Niro do commercials, Times Square has a Disney Store, and I sagged with disappointment at the Academy Awards when I didn't win for directing the best short."

Listening to Griffin, I remember going to plays when I was in film school in New York City in the 1980s. At the time there was a thing known as "the New York actor." These people were occasionally in movies or an episode of *Taxi*, but mostly they were known for theater, and not splashy musical theater, but serious dramas by playwrights like Sam Shepard and Eugene O'Neill. You'd go to tiny theaters in Greenwich Village and tickets were twelve dollars and the plays—many experimental, some of them classic—were really good. At the time a friend gave me a coffee-table book called *Caught in the Act: New York Actors Face to Face*. It's filled with photos of New York stage actors like William Hurt, Kevin Kline, Aidan Quinn, Željko Ivanek, and Griffin.

Now I go to the theater only if someone else pays for the

$180 tickets, and I can't help noticing the playbill is filled with above-the-title movie stars.

As one of those New York actors, Griffin was happy to struggle—to a point. "I was everything but an actor, and I couldn't get a fucking job. I wasn't a good auditioner. I wanted work, I also wanted attention, and I couldn't get work without attention. What's an actor without an audience?"

Just as Griffin was struggling to come to terms with whether or not he would ever have an audience, his New York City roommate and best friend from Los Angeles got a job.

"We lived in a doorman building on the Upper East Side because her mother wanted her to be safe. If her daughter was living in New York, she was going to be in a doorman building. None of this East Village shit, which is what I wanted to do. She was a struggling actress, but much less struggling than me, and her mother was Debbie Reynolds, and Debbie paid half of our rent."

"Oh." I chuckle. "How did things work out for her?"

"One night I came home and I had a bunch of change and crumpled dollars and I'm laying them out, and she says to me— she being Carrie Fisher—'Listen, I got this job and I'm going to be in England for like four months.' 'Congratulations,' I said. She said, 'Oh, it's so stupid—wait until you read the script. It's so dumb!' I said, 'Well, we all gotta work.' So we talked on the phone while she was in England. I would ask her how it was going and she would say, 'Oh my God, I'm acting opposite a nine-foot hairy fucking ape and we hold these little ray guns and we're not even on a fucking set—it's like this big green wall behind us.' And I say, 'What's the name of this piece of shit?'

And she says, 'Star Wars.' I said, 'Is that one word? Is it like Staw—Stawoze?' She said, 'No, that's what I thought, too. But it's two words: it's STAR then it's WARS. Wait until you see it—it's a nightmare.' We roared with laughter about this, and I felt like, 'Well, at least I'm not doing that . . . at least I can keep auditioning!"

I almost can't laugh.

"One of the most startling things I saw happen—to a friend and to a friendship and to all of us who were in this little, tight group—was going to the Ziegfeld Theater for the very first showing of Star Wars. It was when Fox saw it for the first time with an audience at a test screening. And for some reason—this was before Twitter or Facebook or anything—I don't even think the expression 'word of mouth' had been invented and these science fiction, Trekkie nerds knew this was 'a moment.' And there was already a huge crowd of people desperate to see this movie. It wasn't even a paid thing; Fox was giving away tickets. And from the moment that movie started—I also don't think I'd ever heard people cheer at a movie screen. I had never seen a reaction as strong as this. I thought it was incredible. And I loved it, too, and was in awe of it like everyone else. And from that moment, the energy that was going toward Carrie was so fucking intense. And we were kids.

"The doormen, Jimmy and Louie, they fucking loved us and thought of us as kids. I remember getting on the elevator and Louie says, 'How are you doing, Mr. Fisher?' I was like, 'You fuckin' with me, Louie? You called me Mr. Fisher.' He was like, 'No, I didn't.' 'Yes, you did!' He says, 'I'm so sorry.' And I realized it was a harbinger of things to come. You can't imagine how fast this all happened. And I didn't handle it well. I would come home from my shift at two in the morning with my tip belt still on and there in the apartment would be James Taylor crying with Paul Simon because Carly Simon had just broken up with him. Don Henley would be doing blow in the other room. I had a tiny bedroom and all the *Saturday Night Live* people were in there. And here I am with my tip belt stacking my quarters in piles, and I thought, 'I gotta get out of here. This is why I left LA.'"

Of course he felt that way. Seeing the power of celebrity to create a famous person right in front of you—your roommate, who was struggling the way you were a few months ago—is startling. They aren't different in and of themselves, yet the world treats them differently, and then soon enough they have to change, too. But you are still the same, except with them, you have to fight to keep things as they were.

"People called me to get through to her, and it was tough. Of course I was happy for her and she was enjoying herself and we had a shitload of fun, but I knew . . . I thought I had already struck out to find my own identity, to get success on my own terms by moving to New York in the first place, and then this. I moved to the Village instead and went through my process."

Griffin Dunne certainly has had his own share of professional success and celebrity. But given that he grew up in this world and understood its drawbacks made his reaction to it, when it came, different from those of others.

When Griffin was in his late twenties he was the star of *After Hours*, a Martin Scorsese film that debuted at the Cannes Film Festival, so the harsh spotlight of fame suddenly shone on Griffin—and it wasn't all good.

THE STARS IN OUR EYES

"There's a certain curse to having people presume they know who you are, especially when you're young and you're not sure who you are yourself. In those times when I've received the absolute most attention, which has been at movie premieres and particularly after *After Hours* at Cannes, I could actually remove myself and go, 'Wow. I've seen this happen a million times to other people. So this is what this is.' It made me anxious. I thought it incredibly distracting."

After that success, Griffin says, "I was being offered all these movies, [but] I decided to produce a movie instead that I wasn't even in—*Running on Empty*, Sidney Lumet's movie. I wasn't consciously like 'I'm better than fame.' I was seriously conflicted and didn't want the responsibility of either becoming more famous or making a decision and making a big turkey and losing it. I also knew early on that as soon as you reach your height of fame, you start your countdown for how much less famous you are going to be from then on. I didn't want to have that countdown. I'll have my own countdown. It drove my agents crazy. The decisions I made, which at the time seemed so destructive or immature—they were so disparate and illogical—now people think I made some really brilliant, fascinating choices or that I have had this incredibly diverse career, which I'm very proud of. But it was really ruled by neurosis." Still, his fame was on a reasonable level, and he has seen the unreasonable.

"When I starred in a movie opposite Madonna [1987's *Who's That Girl*], it was interesting because it was really an opportunity to think 'That's what fame is!' At the end of the day you have to get in a car that's not your car—it's the follow car so you can fool the people chasing you. Or you're shooting a scene outdoors and you're going to have to reloop the scene [re-record the dialogue] because six helicopters are overhead. Wherever you go, you can't go anywhere. She handled it great, but it was in no way appealing to me.

"I remember we were shooting on a Sunday and it was the New York marathon and we were shooting on Fifth Avenue, which they shut down for the movie. We were right by the park at the end zone of the finishing line. To get crowds of people in New York to watch a movie being made means it must be really something. The crowds build and build, and I noticed they had numbers on them—you know, the marathon numbers. Nobody knew who I was, so I asked one guy what his time was. And he said, 'I didn't finish.' I couldn't believe it. The finish line was literally two hundred yards away and he was not going to cross it! And he said, 'I heard they were filming this movie and Madonna was here and I wanted to watch.' I was like, 'Fucking finish the race—the finish line is right there!'"

I understand the anger and frustration that Griffin felt—that fame is a distraction, that (to quote Julia Roberts's character in *Notting Hill*) "the fame thing isn't really real." But I'm with the runner: the pull of celebrity is stronger than that of any finish line. There are dozens of marathons to run every year, but to watch a real celebrity like Madonna make a movie? That's a once-in-a-lifetime opportunity.

When Griffin's daughter, Hannah, was young, a family friend who was a casting director called him and his then wife, Carey Lowell, about their daughter auditioning. "He said, 'I'm desperate for your daughter to come in and read for *Lemony Snicket*.' Which was Hannah's favorite book series at the time. He told

THE STARS IN OUR EYES

us, 'If she gets it, she gets to go to London for six months with Jim
Carrey. Doesn't that sound like fun?' I thought, 'Fun'?! Am I
going to walk around with my thermos and my little chair and
make sure she has her special meals on set? I don't think so. Let
her get it on her own fucking time . . . She's not going to become
a child actress and then go through all that shit when it's all over
and the PAs aren't bringing you breakfast burritos every morning. I've seen that a million fucking times. She was about eight or
nine years old. I wouldn't tell her, but somehow she found out
and I was furious. We got through it when she realized neither of
her parents was going to give up their own lives so she could live
a dream neither one of us wanted her to have then. I said to her,
'You give me college and get some real life in you and I will help
you out and help you with any resources I have and support you.'
And she did. She's incredibly creative, and the subject she ma-
jored in she dove right into. My secret hope was she would get
incredibly turned on by anthropology and announce, 'I want to
live in Papua New Guinea.' I would have been thrilled . . . Or be
a writer . . . or something like that."

"Something that's not an actress," I suggest.

"When you're a girl and a young actress and pretty, it sort of
becomes 'when are you going to take that fucking thing off?'"
Griffin says, motioning to portray the removal of clothes.

"I saw it all the time, and the pain they went through, and I
didn't want to see my kid go through it. She hasn't been acting
for very long, but I'm happy to tell you she's gotten three jobs in
the past three days. I don't think I've been happier for her in my
whole life. I was having breakfast in Studio City when she called

me to tell me she was going to be on that Louis C.K. show [*Horace and Pete*]. I was like Mama Fuckin' Rose. A sound came out of me and I realized . . . I wasn't just happy for her; I knew she'd bought another day of not being rejected."

With every job, Hannah is staving off her countdown.

"The people who are in it the longest are in it because those feelings don't go away. They learn how to manage them, hopefully, but that's how they sort of survive. Other people say, 'I can't live with the up-and-down of it and defining my self-esteem and my identity whether I get a job or not.' The stakes just go higher. It's the same fucking pain."

I ask Griffin about his father's encouragement.

"He knew how much I wanted it, and it was my mother who said, 'There's no way I'm going to have a kid be in the movie business.' To which I was very angry, and then very grateful later on. A guy came to our house when I was about eight. I had my baseball glove and was going to meet some kid. It was Marty Ritt, and he started asking me questions, which grown-ups on first meeting don't do with eight-year-old kids. When I was leaving, he said to my father, 'Dominick, that kid would be perfect for a movie called *The Reivers* starring opposite Steve McQueen.' McQueen was my favorite, favorite, *favorite*. My idol.

"Dad, who is an excitable guy, told me. He should've talked to my mother first, who would've said don't ever tell him—that's why I knew how to handle the Lemony Snicket thing. When my mother said no, I think I was angry at her for a year. I remember the movie coming out and going to it and thinking, 'That should have been my part!' In my mind, I let down Steve

McQueen and he missed the best opportunity of his professional life."

Griffin says, "I've always had ambivalent feelings about
fame, and I try to know the difference between fame and success. It's always incredibly important to be respected by people
and get respected back. That was a really intoxicating by-product
of fame or success. Having been around it and seen it—I also
knew enough about it to actually have it scare me, too. I didn't
see—with the exception of my father, who didn't see it until well
into his fifties—I didn't see it make anyone happy. I never saw
any real good come from walking into a room and having people go [*he opens his eyes wide in excitement and surprise*]. It fucks
your head up. When people tell you about the greatest points in
their life, it's not going to be 'the night I was at my most famous
and making ten million dollars a movie.' It was probably the
most confusing and complicated time, because you don't really
know who to trust or who you are. You really need to have some
serious fuckin' bones to chart those waters and make it look ef-
fortless, because if you don't, then you're a movie star million-
aire who's complaining about it."

Intermission 5

*The first celebrity I laid eyes on was Jack Lemmon. I was
about seven. I saw him at Sardi's, where I'd been taken by
my parents on a day trip to New York from Philadelphia. My
father spotted him—Lemmon was sitting at a table eating*

lunch just like a regular person—and I was thrilled. The next day I told all my friends. "Who's Jack Lemmon?" someone asked. I had no idea. It didn't matter.

—PATRICIA MARX

★

One day in the late 1970s, my best friend Peter and I pulled up to the curb in front of Junior's Deli on Westwood Boulevard. As we pulled forward into the space, a man frantically jumped out of the car in front of us and approached Peter's window. 'Hey, you guys, I'm leaving, but there's thirty minutes left in the meter, so you should pull up and take it.' 'OK, thanks,' Peter replied. The man jumped into his car and sped away. Peter and I took a beat, looked at each other, and said almost simultaneously, 'Holy shit! That was Mel Brooks!'"

—KELLY CARLIN

★

Elevator story #1, I'm five years old. My pop belonged to something called the Lone Star Boat Club that was literally next door to Studio 54. It was an eight- or nine-floor gentleman's club that skewed Broadway in its membership and allowed Jews in. He would take me there when he wanted to work out (they had squash courts). And he would basically let me loose with the understanding that I would not leave the building or bother anybody. There was a rarely used billiards table in the basement where I would amuse myself. Once I got in the tiny coffin-like elevator, the kind where you needed to open a swinging door, then wait for the inner door to slide open. I got on in the basement. It stopped on the first floor. And Ed Sullivan got on. I knew immediately who he was. We used to watch his TV show every Sunday night. And I would be allowed to stay up until he said good night to his little (racist) mouse character Topo Gigio. Anyway, Ed gets on and it's just the two of us. The doors close and the elevator begins to rise. Past the second floor. Then, a jolt and we stop. Suddenly. Between the second and third floor. And Ed begins to panic. He glares down at me and grunts out, "Were you going to the second floor?" I froze. And even though I wasn't (my dad was on the eighth floor playing squash), I meekly said "yes."

Then Ed blew up. "Then why the hell didn't you push the button, you little shit bastard?" (That's a direct quote I remember to this day.) He called me a slew of other things. Pounded on the door. Pushed the alarm.

And I retreated to the corner of this little lift until help arrived.

When we were freed, he harrumphed away. I found my dad and told him that he needed to beat up Ed Sullivan. My dad hugged me and said that's not how the world works.

★

Elevator story #2, years later: I'm fourteen. My mom gets me and a friend on some inside list to go watch the final dress rehearsal for Saturday Night Live. *I got to cut the audience line and use a special elevator heading up to SNL.*

Tom Snyder climbs on a few floors below. He's jabbering

to somebody about how horrible his time slot was for a prime-time interview show he was then doing on Saturday night. I think it aired at 9 p.m. He was complaining and complaining about his slot. "I'm up against Fantasy Island." *(I think it was* Fantasy Island. *It might have been* The Love Boat.*) He kept on and on until the elevator stopped at his floor. As he got off he said, "You'd have to be an asshole to watch my show."*

I actually did watch his show, so I muttered, "I watch your show, Mr. Snyder."

And he turned back to me as the elevator doors were closing and barked, "Then you're an asshole."

—ALEC SOKOLOW

SIX

A LOVE-HATE CONVERSATION ABOUT THE ARTIST

★

When I was in high school, I wanted to be a character in a Woody Allen movie, if not *actually* Woody Allen. I wanted to move to Manhattan, listen to Louis Armstrong, have a therapist, go to Elaine's, and be acceptably neurotic, maybe even get paid for it.

It's fair to say I had a lot invested in Woody Allen. Since I was a Jewish girl in a WASPy town, he gave me someone to become. Because as blond as I dyed my hair, as many layers of polos, button-downs, and monogrammed sweaters as I put on, I was never going to be of *Town & Country*. But I had a very good shot at a spread in *Shtetl & Ghetto*.

It's difficult for a fan who feels emotionally invested in some-body famous—an actor, a musician, even a politician—when you hear about other aspects of their lives that are not so admirable. That happened to me with Woody Allen. In 1992, Woody Allen admitted to being in love with Mia Farrow's daughter Soon-Yi Previn, who was then twenty-one. He was also accused of molesting his and Mia's daughter Dylan and charges were brought against him. I remember seeing Mia Farrow's other daughter Daisy on the news. She was getting into a station wagon and the reporters had chased her. She gave a supportive comment about her mother and rode off. And I guess I didn't think of it too much. Well, I thought it was gross that Woody was involved with Soon-Yi. Over the next months I saw Woody and Mia going to court, heard his statements, and ultimately watched Mia gain full custody and the rest of the case be dropped. I still went to see his movies, but I really felt the irony in his *Manhattan Murder Mystery* joke about not wanting to listen to Wagner because he gets the urge to conquer Poland.

Nothing today is the same as it was pre-internet, pre–social media. Today famous people tweet and Instagram and Facebook post, and people tweet and Instagram and Facebook post about them, so that any blunders, faux pas, or transgressions are blasted all over the world in seconds and captured in perpetuity. It's like we're drowning in information about celebrities. And the famous have lost control of their fame.

So we have to ask the question: How do we separate the artist from the art? Or can we? Can we separate the fame from the artist? Do we ignore the actor's idiotic tweet and go see their movie anyway?

I remember when I was young, being in my family kitchen in Katonah, New York, and my mother was playing Seals and Crofts on her boom box. My aunt Mattie picked up the cassette case and said, "Uch, don't listen to them. They're anti-abortion." I really love Seals and Crofts and I think about that every time I hear them.

Aunt Mattie is an expert on celebrity. For almost as long as I've known her, she has had subscriptions to *People, Us Weekly*, and every tabloid known to man (and the subscriptions read "Dr. Mattie Matthews" because her sister found that doctors get discounts on magazines); she regularly watches *Entertainment Tonight* and *Access Hollywood* and is a devotee of TMZ, Celebitchy, and other entertainment sites. If there were a PhD in celebrity information, Mattie would not only have it, but she'd also be directing thesis students. (So the Dr. designation isn't so far off.)

I cannot tell you how many times over the years I've mentioned a celebrity and Mattie has shot a stinging arrow of judgment at him or her: "wife abuser," "adulterer," and "deadbeat dad." So much so that she has trained me to do it. When my boyfriend, Dan, told me a moving story from his childhood about growing up on a farm in Iowa and listening to Glen Campbell's "Wichita Lineman," I said, "Didn't he beat up Tanya Tucker?" thus ruining someone else's childhood memory.

He's begged me not to do this. But I can't help it. When I have important information about a celebrity, good or bad, I feel it is my duty as a citizen of the republic of celebrity to share it.

Mattie and I are very close, even though she's as different from her sister (my mother) as she can be. My parents have had an organic garden since the early 1970s and now live in rural New England, while Mattie used to drink Pepsis while smoking True Blues and eating Entenmann's donuts in Midtown

Manhattan (these days she no longer smokes and drinks Diet Pepsi). I remember one night when I was about fifteen and all of us went out to dinner. The waiter asked my parents, "Baked potato, mashed potato, or fries?" Their response was, "No potatoes." Mattie looked at them and said, "I've never in my life heard those words uttered." I looked at her and said, "Now do you know how I feel?" From that moment on, we were a bonded unit.

Recently we went to our psychopharmacologist (we go together, so I only get charged for half a session).

We have our appointment at 11 a.m. so we can go straight to lunch after (someplace with a wine list) and together solve the problems of the world. This time I asked her for her thoughts on whether it's possible to separate the artist from the work. Can you do it? Can you enjoy a famous person's movies when he's been accused of being a sexual predator? Can you love watching a professional athlete on the field when you know he's been accused of abusing his wife?

As well as being an expert in celebrity culture, Mattie is also a former social worker. She understands that how people act in public isn't necessarily how they act in private, and that the court of public opinion isn't always right.

"Have you ever bought an album or seen a movie of a famous person you hate personally?" I asked.

It seemed to me that to really answer the question, it had to be directed at a celebrity whose work you value. For example, Mattie and I hated Justin Bieber over the monkey incident. (In 2013 he had a young capuchin monkey as a pet and brought it with him on tour to Germany, where it was quarantined because Bieber didn't have the proper documentation. When he was done performing in Germany, he just left the monkey there.) In all honesty, our protest of Justin Bieber wouldn't make a dent in his sales, since neither of us could even name a single song of his and have never spent a dime buying any of them.

There are plenty of celebrities I have huge disdain for, which usually means I don't care about their art on any level. I used to love John Travolta but in recent years his involvement with Scientology as well as the whole "Adele Dazeem" thing (when he mispronounced Idina Menzel's name while introducing her at the 2014 Oscars) have made him unpalatable to me. Mattie thinks it's because I'm creeped out by his hair. I think it may be the fact that he's making movies I really don't want to see.

With Tom Cruise, on the other hand, I feel like I can separate his professional life from his personal idiosyncrasies. Over the years I've heard some troubling stories about him— yes, gossip—but they would not keep me from seeing a Tom Cruise movie. In fact, he's one of the few stars I pay twenty bucks to watch on the big screen. I think he's a great actor and anytime I've seen him be himself, like when he did the ALS Ice Bucket Challenge on YouTube, I have really liked him. (I didn't like his anti-antidepressant rant, but that wasn't a deal breaker for me.)

For Aunt Mattie and me, Woody Allen represents a perfect example of the conflict between art and artist.

I liked him because I thought he made it cool to be Jewish. But once I started to read stories about Mariel Hemingway saying that Woody Allen was lechy during the filming of *Manhattan*, I felt more like a woman than a Jew and thought, "That's enough for me." I stopped seeing his movies and even began to have a hard time with my old favorites of his, which for me is a truly great loss.

Mattie and I also discussed that there are certain people whom we want to defend and like because they've meant something to us for a long time—the way my boyfriend wants to defend Glen Campbell.

The other issue is, what is the act? There are crimes that I (and Mattie) find unforgivable. They range from any sort of animal cruelty (Bieber, Michael Vick) to the following (ordered from least offensive to most):

- Screaming at your kids (Alec Baldwin, but I've forgiven him now)
- Being very conservative politically (Adam Baldwin, James Woods, Scott Baio)
- Having damaging political opinions (Susan Sarandon calling Hillary Clinton a liar)
- Being a racist (Paula Deen, Flannery O'Connor)
- Drugging and raping women (Bill Cosby, allegedly)
- Having inappropriate sexual contact with kids (Stephen Collins)
- Committing murder (O. J. Simpson, allegedly)
- Being Donald Trump!

(As I write this book, more than fifty women have come forward to allege that Bill Cosby sexually assaulted them. Though I've heard stories about Cosby's behavior, I wondered if for many people in the black community, Bill Cosby was like Woody Allen was for American Jews. *The Cosby Show* was groundbreaking, and his character, Dr. Cliff Huxtable, was an African American, upper-middle-class professional; this was not Fred Sanford or even George Jefferson. This was something very different.)

I realize a lot of people are defending these celebrities and their actions. Ironically enough, I remember Woody Allen as Alvy Singer in *Annie Hall* recalling the joke about the guy who thinks his brother's a chicken, but he won't turn him in because he needs the eggs. Alvy compares that to relationships: "We all need the eggs."

I think that is true for our relationships with celebrities as well. We need the celebrities we like and admire to be better than we are, to dazzle us with their talent, to make us laugh and cry and cheer. If they do that, whether they're on the screen or onstage or on the basketball court or football field, we put them on pedestals. But when they disappoint us, we're crushed. We're angry and hurt and we feel foolish that we ever believed in them in the first place.

That was never more clear than with our first Tweeter in chief, Donald Trump. Whether you embraced his social media posts or were appalled by them, the fact is that until his election, Americans had never seen this kind of communication before. He is the first American president to use Twitter to funnel his unfiltered thoughts out to the world. And that became a problem for people who want their leaders to speak in measured tones after having thought long and hard about complex issues, and discussed them with their advisors, who are experts on foreign policy, diplomacy, and constitutional law. Being famous, powerful, and unfiltered can be a worrying combination for many people.

What it comes down to, I suppose, is that with celebrity, we all have our own lines in the sand. I can never really separate the artist from the art, because part of the art has to do with the creation of it and what or who is behind it. I guess I'd just rather do without the eggs.

Intermission 6

The summer of 2002 had been particularly hot, and I hadn't been out of the house since I gave birth to our daughter, Lucia, in June. My husband, Tim, knew it would take something drastic to lure me out of the nursery and back out into the world. He knew he'd have to go big. He'd have to go Bruce.

As the lighting designer at Late Show with David Letterman, *Tim invited me to watch the rehearsal of Bruce Springsteen and the E Street Band, who were set to appear to promote* The Rising. *For the first time since Lucia was born, I dressed, put on makeup, and got in a cab.*

That afternoon, cars were bumper to bumper on the West Side Highway. The driver navigated as best as he could through the traffic, pulling up to a stoplight around 30th Street. The cars were three across at the stoplight; ahead, nothing but gridlock. Marooned, I looked over and saw a man on the street corner juggling. He wasn't juggling normal objects, like balls, but three disparate objects: a large glass bottle, a broken umbrella (open with wonky spokes), and some kind of serving utensil.

Mesmerized by his skill, I fished in my purse and pulled out some money. I leaned out the window and waved to him. The juggler smiled and came my way. I thanked him. Together, we heard the whirl of an automatic window in the next vehicle, a shiny black SUV. We looked up, saw a hand holding a generous bill, and finally, as the window came down completely, we saw the face of Bruce Springsteen. He smiled at the juggler, who took his money and went on to the next car. Then Bruce smiled at me. I tried to speak. My arms went out the cab window to reach for him. I must have looked like one of those desperate sinners in the Renaissance paintings of Italian masters, flailing to be rescued as they fry in the flames of hell. I wanted to tell him what his music meant to me or just to say, How about this heat? *But before I could, his window went up and the vehicle peeled away.*

—ADRIANA TRIGIANI

★

My parents used to live in the same building as Paul Simon, and occasionally we'd share an elevator ride with him. Once, when it was just me, Paul, and my mother, she complimented him on his eyeglasses chain. He said, "I have more just like it—here, you have it." And he took the chain from around his neck and gave it to her, just like that. Their next memorable elevator encounter was on 9/11. Shortly after the towers were hit, my mother went outside to walk our dog. She ran into

Paul in the lobby and asked whether he was going to get his son, who was in grade school at the time. In her words, "He looked at me like I had two heads and said, 'Do you even KNOW what's going ON??? We're at WAR!'"

—MERRILL STUBBS

★

Several winters ago I was walking up Broadway in a typically unjustified cranky mood when I noticed a man walking straight toward me. He was looking down, not paying attention, as he put on a pair of leather gloves. The gloves struck me as kind of fancy-looking, almost elegant. For reasons that a hundred psychiatrists on their best day could never crack, the fancy gloves just pissed me off more. Anyway, he wasn't watching where he was going and he was about to walk into me when I barked out, "Watch it, watch, it, watch it." You know, rapid-fire and obnoxious. The man quickly stopped and looked up . . . and I found myself face-to-face with the great Frank Langella, who looked rather lost and melancholy. Then, in the warmest, most sincere, and unpretentiously fancy voice I'd ever heard, said, "I'm terribly sorry." I felt like a gigantic asshole. To make matters worse, I realized it had only been two days since he'd lost the Oscar for his performance in Frost/Nixon *to Sean Penn . . . and now he's getting dissed on Broadway by a slob like me.*

—ALAN SMITHEE

SEVEN

THE WAY WE WERE AND ARE

Celebrity Then and Now

★

You can't really talk about the nature of celebrity without talking about how things have changed. "Old Hollywood" or "the golden age of baseball" means something to a lot of people. For many, it means a better time, whether or not it really was. Such as when movie stars were not "just like us." That's when I think about *Sunset Boulevard*—I could quote the entire movie here because pretty much everything that's said in it relates to this idea:

"I *am* big. It's the *pictures* that got small."

"They took the idols and smashed them, the Fairbankses, the Gilberts, the Valentinos! And who've we got now? Some nobodies!"

"No one ever leaves a star. That's what makes one a star."

And on and on and on.

And although I am a devoted fan of every Fred and Ginger movie, and Preston Sturges, Frank Capra, Howard Hawks, William Wyler, Billy Wilder, *The Wizard of Oz*, etc., I have to admit that I am more fascinated by 1970s Hollywood than any other era. The images of Hollywood glamour in the '30s and '40s feel very staged to me, and I've seen them only in newsreels. But the '70s feel more real, and a little closer. I was a kid then; it isn't ancient history.

Once I was at dinner with my agent, Esther Newberg, and her friend (who is now my friend) the producer Diane Sokolow. They were talking about the Business in the 1970s—mostly about their friend and Esther's fellow International Creative Management (ICM) superagent, the late Sue Mengers. Mengers represented Candice Bergen, Peter Bogdanovich, Michael Caine, Cher, Joan Collins, Brian De Palma, Faye Dunaway, Bob Fosse, Gene Hackman, Sidney Lumet, Mike Nichols, Nick Nolte, Burt Reynolds, and Barbra Streisand. Mengers herself embodied larger-than-life Hollywood. She's been profiled in *Vanity Fair*, and Bette Midler starred in a one-woman show about her. In his memoriam for her, *Vanity Fair* editor Graydon Carter wrote, "Sue Mengers died in mid-October [2011] at her home, a short walk from the Beverly Hills Hotel, surrounded by three of her close friends, Ali MacGraw, Joanna Poitier, and Boaty Boatwright."

I told Esther and Diane how I would've loved to have interviewed Sue Mengers. At about the same moment, Diane and Esther said, "Oh, then you must talk to Michael Black."

"Who is he?" I asked.

"He was an agent, now he's a manager," Esther explained.

Diane said, "You just turn on your tape recorder and let him talk."

In the reception area of Michael Black's office on Wilshire Boulevard, there was a big bowl of sparkly candies, which reminded me of one of my favorite things that I'd heard about Sue Mengers: that she called movie stars "sparklies."

When I explained the idea behind this book, Michael Black pointed to the differences between being famous in the old days and fame today.

"First of all," he said, "we never would have been talking about this then. They would never discuss this in the era when we had stars. Outside of Hedda Hopper and Louella Parsons, everything was controlled by the studios. People didn't have TVs and they couldn't see the stars in public without a script. The players had their wardrobe departments dressing them for fabulous premieres, and the studios would pay Hedda to say someone other than Rock Hudson was gay and ruin that person's career. Now when you see these famous actors—these poor stars! If they want to keep up their image, they have to get dressed up to go to Starbucks.

"Back then the Oscars used to be fun because the people dressed themselves, so they'd have ridiculous outfits and hairdos. Now they all have stylists. Little kids have stylists because their parents want endorsements. It's all business."

The ups and downs of actors' careers go hand in hand with their celebrity. "The careers that last are the ones that started hot, then they had their lean period, and then they came back and they appreciate it all. Any star that is going to be a star goes through a cold period. People forget that Meryl Streep didn't work for a long time after *She-Devil* with Roseanne Barr. She couldn't even make a TV movie of the week. Everyone has had their lean periods and some of them hang around and get re-birthed."

Black was from Long Island, a suburban New Yorker like me. I wondered if he'd always wanted to be in show business.

"My father turned me on to showbiz by taking me to Broadway as a kid," Black said. "He ran the Dean Martin and Jerry Lewis telethon, so I would always get the autographs. When I grew up, I went to college and found boring preppies just discovering grass. I knew I didn't want to be a doctor—a lot of people in my family were doctors. So I became a lawyer."

Though he settled on becoming a lawyer, Black's interest in entertainment was always there. "I used to act," he said. "I remember one audition, the call was for a twenty-year-old collegiate guy. I was in college. The fellow said it was for a cola commercial. Try it, the director said, do it however you want. All the guys went up with their cans and were all gorgeous, and I thought, 'I can't compete with these guys.' So I went up there and gave them a little personality—you know, the screw-you attitude. The guy I thought was the casting director said, 'Hey, schmuck, you've been waiting this whole time—you sure you don't want to try again?' I said 'No. I wanted to give you some personality.' Another guy who I didn't realize was the casting director said, 'That's the guy I want.' And I got the commercial.

What I learned from that and what I passed on to my actor clients is that if you really want something, say you really want it, but don't be desperate. No one likes the scarlet letter *H*—for *hunger*—on your forehead. It was an eye-opener for me because I was on my day off from lifeguarding when I auditioned. If I had been a forty-year-old-guy with the wife and baby who needed the job—it was a national commercial—I wonder if I would have had the balls to do what I did."

Black's transition to show business after law school came about through luck more than intent. "After I finished law school, I ended up in New York doing bankruptcy law and hated it. I had never been to California, and in 1973 I went out to visit my roommate from law school, who was working at Universal. We went to dinner and by some weird bit of fate, a guy I knew from Georgetown was at his house and he said, 'Michael, you want to go into entertainment law?' I said, 'Yeah, sure.' He was becoming a music agent that day for a company called CMA. I had never heard of CMA or thought of applying to an agency. He said there's going to be an opening and they have a New York office. I said great. I do the interview and forget about it and two weeks later it's Labor Day. I get the call Labor Day of 1973—can you come out here? I didn't ask what I was making: $12,005! I had just gotten a raise in New York and then I went down to $12,005. It was the only thing in my life I ever did on chance.

"So I'm in LA dealing with all the entertainment firms and I passed the California bar and I notice all the attorneys were telling their clients what movies to take, and I thought, 'I can do this.'

"Back then Freddie Fields, the original überagent, ruled the coop with an iron hand, and said, 'I don't want their outside attorneys to see the contract until it's perfected in-house.'"

Michael looked out the window now. "I'm sure every generation says it and I'm sure it's a sign of age, but it really was better back then. It was so much fun, and then William Morris came in and it became suits and the flamboyant agents like Sue [Mengers] began to die. It's business, business, business. Back then it was a big thing to ask for a million—very rare to get a million. Then to live through an era where Harrison Ford gets twenty-five million dollars or Mel Gibson gets twenty million dollars. Now we're back in an era where they're cutting actors again and cutting net profits."

There's a big difference, too, in what it takes to be a celebrity, Black said. "Movie stars didn't do TV. Very few made the transition. Clint Eastwood in *Rawhide*—he had to go make spaghetti westerns to make a name here. Movie stars didn't do TV commercials. Unheard of! Stars didn't do endorsements. You didn't see stars walk down catwalks or an Oscar nominee endorsing Coach. It's all branding now—there wasn't branding back then. Now there's the idea that you, too, can have this perfume, fashion lines. It's big business." It seems to me that it's almost essential to be doing something other than acting: endorsing a perfume or attaching yourself to a charity or creating a lifestyle brand. Celebrities are rarely just actors anymore.

I asked him if there's anything positive about show business today. And he said, "The good news is you can still be an unknown, open on Broadway, and become a star overnight. It hasn't happened recently, but it can. Remember Jennifer Holliday in *Dreamgirls*? She became a star overnight on Broadway.

"Sometimes it happens on TV. Look at these people on *Game of Thrones*. They're stars overnight and it's pretty amazing. There are only two industries where you can literally be playing stickball in the street and making millions a few years later: sports and show business. Not politicians, because they have to kiss a lot of ass to be a star.

"I've seen both sides. I've represented the Bette Davises, the Gregory Pecks, Astaires, Katharine Hepburns toward the end of their careers and saw how they were dealing with it. Bette wasn't ready to retire—she was ready to work always. I loved working with Astaire. I got him in a movie that he won an Emmy for opposite Helen Hayes. He was so proud of it and said, 'If my mother could see me now.' He didn't do one dance number. It was interesting to see them at the end of their careers and not taking the lead. Humbling. Like Bette Davis—I got her to do a voice-over for Equal. She loved it. Did it in half an hour—two takes—made fifty thousand dollars. She said, 'Jack [Warner], eat your heart out. I did twenty movies for fifty thousand dollars.'"

I asked him about the differences between stars then and now in the information age, and he said, "When Audrey Hepburn made a million for *My Fair Lady* or Elizabeth Taylor got a million for *Cleopatra*, that was news. But you didn't know what the other stars were making. Now everyone's salary is in the news. You can see what they're making and how much their house cost . . . I mean Honey Boo Boo is making more money than anyone . . . It's staggering.

"Celebrity has changed. These yentas in Jersey, these mob wives are celebrities. People don't know where Canada is, but they know the circumference of Kim Kardashian's ass. And you see Justin Bieber's mom putting his little video online and then now that little pip-squeak makes sixty million dollars a year. When I heard that, I wondered, should I be handing out my business cards at Toys 'R' Us?"

Everybody's heard stories about stars making incredible demands. For example, I once heard that Kim Basinger had cases of Evian water delivered to a set for washing her hair. But my favorite celebrity demands are the leaked backstage riders in performers' contracts. Like Beyoncé, who enjoys "Juicy Baked Chicken: Legs, Wings & Breast only (Please season with fresh garlic, season salt, black pepper, and Cayenne pepper HEAVILY SEASONED!!)," and Adele, who demands good red wine and Marlboro Lights. Rihanna wants white drapes to cover anything ugly in her dressing room, and Katy Perry wants flower arrangements that must be pink fresh flowers. "White and purple hydrangeas, pink & white roses and peonies. If not available, seasonal white flowers to include white orchids—ABSOLUTELY NO CARNATIONS."

I asked Michael if that happened in the 1970s. "That's when it started," he said, "I remember helping Freddie Fields and the huge deal with Steve McQueen for *Papillon*. I had never seen a miscellaneous section in a contract before. [McQueen] would have his barber flown to wherever he was every three weeks. His weights and motorbikes had to be transported to every location. Fourteen round-trip tickets so his friends could visit him. Now they want separate trailers for workout equipment or one for the nanny and kids.

"Steve Ross, the CEO of Warner Communications, used to treat his stars fabulously with the private plane or the house in Mexico. I remember the *Lethal Weapon* team giving Range Rovers to Mel Gibson and Danny Glover after it was big. But you don't hear stuff like that now.

"It's changed so much. The fact that you can be an unknown kid—like when you see the *Twilight* stars. Taylor Lautner got eight million, and now he's probably saying, 'Paper or plastic?' That's celebrity."

Celebrity is fleeting. In a few rare cases it lasts, but not without excruciating attention, magnificent guidance, luck, and an ability to adapt to changing styles and tastes. For most of the rest, however, it can feel like fame lasts for about fifteen minutes.

Intermission 7

Bedford, New York, is a bucolic village suburb north of New York City where I moved my family so that my two young children could enjoy the fresh air, the woods, and the wonderful public schools. It's also where Glenn Close's character boils somebody's bunny rabbit in Fatal Attraction. *Anyway, she must have been taken with the town, because after the movie she moved there, too.*

Shortly after filming her starring role as Cruella De Vil in 101 Dalmatians, *Ms. Close graciously arranged for a complimentary screening for all the children and families of Bedford Village Elementary.*

That was the good news.

The Bedford Playhouse is a sweet one-screen movie theater. The screening was to take place on a Saturday, and in order for everybody to attend we had to fill this small theater in shifts, as assigned. My family had the 8 a.m. show.

It was a freezing winter day. Kids in the front, grown-ups in the back. I'm in the second-to-last row, my friend and neighbor Janie to my left. I had left home in a hurry, without coffee, and was feeling mighty cranky about my assigned screening time and the coin toss I lost with my (then) wife.

"OK, so where the fuck is Glenn Close and when are they starting this piece of shit???!!!" It was a whisper, but it was not my indoor whisper.

A solid boot heel to the top of my foot from Janie . . . "She's sitting right behind you."

—ROBBIE KONDOR

★

When I was pregnant with our first child, we lived in San Francisco. My husband was preparing to leave the law to try his hand at broadcast journalism. Money would be tight. But we wanted to take one last adventuresome trip before our lives would be changed forever by a baby. We planned a low-budget, two-week trip to the Hawaiian islands, staying in a combination of B&Bs and camping.

When we got to the Big Island, we were ready for something more than state park bathrooms and skin-thin towels. Giggling to ourselves, we crashed the beach of a five-star *hotel, buying a few ten-dollar cocktails to justify our squatting. Lo and behold, I spotted Kevin Costner and his then wife cuddling in a cabana and still glowing from* Dances with Wolves *Oscar fame. Just like Scooby-Doo hypnotized by the ghost clown, my brain became immediately obsessed with getting a closer look at that million-dollar grin.*

I am ashamed to admit that it became inexplicably critical that Kevin Costner know I was pregnant. I needed him to understand that the gentle swell of my belly (I was all of four months along) was not due to laziness. Bob and I were joining his club. We loved kids. We were just like him!

Let me just add that the Costners were kind of all over each other in that "whoopeeee, we've left the kids at home" married way. The fact that I believed he would even NO-TICE me is more than a little embarrassing, all these years later.

When his wife got up to go to the bathroom, I followed suit, cradling my belly, timing my exit from the stall to coincide with hers. I no longer remember how I started the conversation as we were washing our hands at the sink. But I made a point to work my pregnancy into the conversation (because that's a natural topic over hand soap). I'm sure she beat a hasty exit, pegging me as some stalker freak. I do remember spending the rest of our time there feeling like I had joined some rarified club. Me and Bob and the Costners, all part of this insider world of parenthood.

—LEE WOODRUFF

★

In 1994, when everyone was talking about Six Degrees of Kevin Bacon, which I thought was really kind of a stupid game, I worked in advertising at Young & Rubicam, on Madison Avenue.

In those days I was an ad exec by day and an aspiring cartoonist at night. I was burning the midnight oil drawing and writing cartoons, trying to achieve the dream. But I was going to work on two hours' sleep and nodding off in client meetings like a junkie. I lived on caffeine.

There was a Dunkin' Donuts down the street from my office, and I left my office half-awake in desperate need of some caffeine. I walked out of DD sipping my extra-large coffee, not looking where I was going, and opened the glass door on to the sidewalk, and all of a sudden I hear a male voice say, "OH, FUCK!" I see papers flying and then an agitated man bending down to pick them up. I apologized because I bumped into him. He looked up. And I found my-self one degree of Kevin Bacon.

—MARISA ACOCELLA MARCHETTO

EIGHT

MY EVOLVING RELATIONSHIP WITH JENNIFER ANISTON

★

I t was a Friday when I heard. My Black Friday.

DATELINE: 01/07/2005 AT 07:00 PM EDT

Hollywood power couple Jennifer Aniston and Brad Pitt have decided to separate, PEOPLE magazine reports exclusively.

"We would like to announce that after seven years together we have decided to formally separate. For those who follow these sorts of things, we would like to explain that our separation is not the result of any of the speculation reported by the tabloid media. This decision is the result of much thoughtful

consideration," Pitt and Aniston said in a joint
statement to PEOPLE magazine. "We happily remain
committed and caring friends with great love and
admiration for one another. We ask in advance for your
kindness and sensitivity in the coming months."

Brad and Jen, my imaginary best friends, my absolute favorite celebrity couple, had split up. Over the next few days they
were on the cover of every entertainment magazine on the
planet. I bought both *People* and *Us Weekly*. There were pictures.
Days before their announcement they had gone on a beach vacation to Anguilla with the Cox-Arquettes. There they were photographed walking on the beach, Brad in a long-sleeve T-shirt
that read "Trash," camouflage shorts, and aviator sunglasses; Jen
in a white tank and pareo. There was one picture of him with his
arm around her, her clutching his hand, him kissing the side of
her head, her brow furrowed. All was not right. In another picture they were actually kissing. They looked heartbroken.

What was happening? I was shattered.

I remember going to my therapist. I walked in and she said,
"Are you OK?"

I wasn't crying, but I looked troubled.

"I know this sounds crazy," I said, "But I am really upset
about Jennifer Aniston and Brad Pitt."

She had a look of curious relief on her face. She shook her
head and said, "You have no idea how many of my clients have
come in and talked about this."

Recently I looked at the pictures again. It's been more than ten years. Since then, my own marriage has broken up, and all four of us have moved on. I have a great boyfriend, and my ex-husband has a lovely girlfriend. Angelina and Brad had their many, many, *many* children before splitting up in 2016 (prompting the hashtag #Brangelexit). I must admit, their divorce didn't really bother me, though I felt bad for their children that their lives were disrupted so publicly, and angry about the memes that circulated at the time, showing a laughing (maybe gloating?) Jennifer Aniston—*as if she would care.* Jen is happily married to the smart *and* hot Justin Theroux. Yet those pictures of Brad and Jen, all these years later, are like a punch in the gut to me. Even today when I look at them, I think, "What went wrong?" Of course the question I should really be asking is *What is wrong with me?*

My obsession with Jennifer Aniston started long before the breakup. I loved her on *Friends.* Rachel was a Long Island Jewish girl who took a long time to find her way (I could relate), and I loved when she let her hair grow long. Oh, those gorgeous locks—that sun-kissed blond and that caramel skin that tans so beautifully, light blue eyes, absolutely perfect bikini body. (And to be clear, I'm straight. My love for Jennifer Aniston has nothing to do with sex.) Even today, I buy any magazine that she's on the cover of and lose myself in the artfully staged and airbrushed glimpses of her life and follow every suggested beauty tip (after applying mascara, blow dry your eyelashes).

I've talked about this obsession with my friend Jancee over the years, because she is very interested in celebrity but doesn't have these kinds of obsessions—together she and I had the best celebrity sighting EH-VER. It was 1997 at Saks Fifth Avenue, where we were lunching and shopping because we were both covering the Grammy Awards. We went into the shoe department and were sitting in chairs when we saw a woman with an all-male entourage. She had her back to us, but we knew we were looking at the First Lady of Soul. She picked up a pair of tiny gold sandals and asked the salesman to bring them in her size. She slipped them on and walked toward us and said, "Cute, right?"

And we said, "Oh, Aretha, they're stunning!"

She giggled and said, "The run in my stockings really makes the look, right?"

Both Jancee and I died.

But mostly, Jancee doesn't have the faux relationships with stars that I do. Occasionally she'll have a picture of someone famous torn from a magazine in her wallet, but it's because she likes the outfit, not the being.

As I thought about why people respond to certain celebrities but not others, I came across an article in *New Scientist* from June 2005 about research on neurons and how we respond to people we recognize (and no, it did not have a picture of Jennifer Aniston on the cover). It read:

"In the 1960s, neuroscientist Jerry Lettvin suggested that people have neurons that respond to a single concept, such as, for example, their grandmother. The notion of these hyperspecific neurons, coined 'grandmother cells,' was quickly rejected by psychologists as laughably simplistic.

"But Rodrigo Quiroga, at the University of Leicester [in the

United Kingdom], who led the new study, and his colleagues recently found some very grandmother-like cells. Previous unpublished findings from the team showed tantalising results: a neuron that fired only in response to pictures of former US president Bill Clinton, or another to images of the Beatles. But for such 'grandmother cells' to exist, they must invariably respond to the 'concept' of Bill Clinton, not just similar pictures.

"To investigate further, the team turned to eight patients currently undergoing treatment for epilepsy. In an attempt to locate the brain areas responsible for their seizures, each patient had around 100 tiny electrodes implanted in their brain. Many of the wires were placed in the hippocampus—an area of the brain vital to long-term memory formation.

"[The researchers] first gave each subject a screening test, showing them between 71 and 114 images of famous people, places, and even food items. For each subject, the researchers measured the electrical activity, or 'firing,' of the neurons connected to the electrodes. Of the 993 neurons sampled, 132 fired to at least one image.

"The team then went back for a testing phase, this time showing participants three to seven different pictures of the initial 132 photo subjects that hit. For example, one woman saw seven different photos of Jennifer Aniston alongside 80 other photos of animals, buildings or additional famous people such as Julia Roberts. The neuron almost [completely] ignored all other photos, but fired steadily each time Aniston appeared on screen."

And that woman was me (no, just kidding, but it could've been).

. . .

It's clear my brain has some kind of special Jennifer Aniston chip in it. And I'm not alone. Year after year, the top-selling issues of US magazines are the ones with Jennifer Aniston on the cover.

I don't often think about my feelings for Jennifer, mainly because I have a very fulfilling life. I'm not looking to escape. Although I guess even the nicest lives can use distraction. Jennifer Garner, herself a beautiful, accomplished celebrity, said in the March 2016 *Vanity Fair,* "When Jen Aniston and Brad Pitt broke up, I was dying to see something that said they were getting back together." Oh, Jennifer Garner, me too!

Caring about the emotional happiness of a celebrity is, I think, a sort of safe emotional escape. It gives us a chance to watch someone else's successful, satisfying, and even romantic life. But I wonder: Why Jen? Why not, say, Charlize Theron, who might be more beautiful than Jen? Maybe that's part of it. Years ago an acquaintance interviewed Angelina Jolie, and I had one of my million how-could-Brad-have-chosen-Angelina-over-Jen conversations with him—the ones where I get waaaaaaay too excited. He had previously interviewed Jen, so he had a truly scientifically balanced perspective.

He said, "Jennifer Aniston is like the beautiful women you see on Madison Avenue. She's one of us." He paused for a moment and said, "Angelina is different. She is one of them." One of *them.* The unapproachable goddesses.

I have never seen Jennifer Aniston in person (and after writing this, I'm fairly sure she won't be inviting me to her beach house for the weekend). But I did see Angelina once at the premiere party for A *Mighty Heart*. She was ethereal, tiny boned, with enormous eyes and lips. She looked to me like, when she was done with the party, a bunch of bluebirds would swoop down and take her away.

And that is why I prefer Jen to Angelina. She would ride the subway, probably holding a big coffee, glued to her phone. Just like me. I see her as an escape that feels closer to my life, my outlook. She might, given the right circumstances (i.e., if she weren't a huge movie star), be my friend. I don't think Angelina would be. I don't think she'd ever want to leave the bluebirds behind and drink wine with me on my fire escape. I don't think I'd want to be friends with Angelina, either. She once cut a boyfriend's name into her arm. That is so not me.

Sandra Bullock once was complimented by an interviewer, and she said, "Oh, you're so sweet. I'm going to get up and hug you." And she did. As she was returning to her chair, she said, "Did the camera get a good shot of my fat ass?" Such a great combination of self-deprecation and compassion for others and an inherent understanding of how celebrity works: instant love from me!

But would I *really* want to be friends with Sandra or Jen? Probably not. I have a couple of good friends who are very close friends with big celebrities, so I have an inkling of what it's actually like. It's not what you think. One of them is friends with a performer who tops the list of people everyone thinks they could be friends with. My friend said this performer loves to lie in bed all day and makes everyone do it with them. It sounds kind of depressing to me. I think it's better for all of us if we normal people watch the famous from a distance, and not have to drink hot lemon water with them.

I believe there is a sense that when we see some celebrities in real time—for example, dating, traveling together, sneaking make-out sessions, going for a cup of coffee in sweats and UGGs—it's almost like we are watching a movie and we want a happy ending. For others, like the ones we love to hate (cough Kardashians cough), it's more fun to place bets on the expiration dates of their relationships. She can't stay married for more than thirty days. She might have more money than Croesus, but she can't maintain a relationship.

After my daughter was born, I was having a load of trouble: my health was bad, my baby was too small, our finances were a wreck, I remember seeing pictures in magazines of Brooke Shields with her new baby in her fantastic home and thinking how lucky she was. I had a tiny one-bedroom apartment with my baby in a very used basinet beside my bed. Brooke was sure to have a giant nursery and a slew of baby nurses and people cleaning her house and cooking her delicious, healthy meals. And while that may have been true, I learned later that she suffered from severe postpartum depression. I don't think I would have wanted to know that at the time. I liked imagining her having a positive experience: an easy labor, a quick recovery, a smooth transition into happy, satisfying motherhood. And although I was still happily married in 2005 when Jen and Brad split up, I wonder now if there were subconscious inklings that something like that was coming for me. Otherwise, why would I have cared so much? Why is it so painful to revisit the photos now?

For the most part I've moved on. I don't wake up in the middle of the night and think what could have been with Jen and Brad. Some of my obsession has faded. Now I find myself coveting shots of amazing-looking women who are older than me. That's my new celebrity obsession. Oh, and the Obamas. I like to think it's a mature step and being a fan of a gorgeous, smart, funny, insightful, former president and first lady says something about how my character has deepened. But really, I think it's just a lateral move.

Intermission 8

I did a radio tour for the publication of my novel. I sat in a studio and was interviewed by DJs and talk show hosts in radio stations all over the country.

Most of the interviewers were nice. The most interesting question: What's it like having Dennis Miller mouthing off around the house all the time? I said that I imagined it would be a living hell, though I could only venture a guess, as I've never met Dennis Miller. The poor man had just spent ten minutes thinking he was interviewing Dennis Miller's wife. He began stammering his apologies and it became clear that he had no idea whose wife it was that he was interviewing, and I felt so sorry for him that I ended up repeatedly apologizing to him for not being Dennis Miller's wife.

When I got home I told my Denis—Denis Leary—about it and he insisted that I have met Dennis Miller and I said that wasn't Dennis Miller, it was Jay Mohr, and Denis be-

came very annoyed because I really never have any idea who anyone is.

Once, I was seated next to Moby at a dinner party. This was years ago and I had spent the summer listening to a Moby CD that Denis had made me, but I had no idea what Moby looked like. So at this dinner party, I was seated next to a very sweet, slightly nebbishy-looking guy who seemed a little out of his element. Meg Ryan was there, Jon Stewart, Nora Ephron. I think the party was for Barry Levinson. Anyway, my sweet dinner companion was concerned that there wouldn't be anything for him to eat, as he was a vegan. He was just so quiet and unassuming that I realized he was probably overwhelmed by the dazzling luminaries in the room and I decided to take him under my wing. I asked one of the wait-staff to prepare him a salad and then I explained to him who all the important people were. At one point I asked him what he did for work. He told me that he was a musician. "How nice," I said, imagining him in an orchestra pit, his upper lip quivering above a flute, or perhaps on a subway platform strumming on a mandolin. When we left the party, Denis and I shared a ride with Jon Stewart and his wife, Tracey.

"What was Moby like?" Tracey asked.

"Moby was there?" I asked, in all my innocence.

—ANN LEARY

★

Many years ago I was strolling through Greenwich Village eating colorful jelly beans from a crisp white bag when I *looked up and there she stood. Carole King. She was on the corner of Sixth Avenue and 8th Street. She was corralling two very cute young children, presumably her grandchildren, a boy and a girl.*

I had seen her several years earlier when we both stood at a red light, waiting to cross a street. At that time I said hello and she was so warm and gracious when she said hello back to me! AND, she even wished me luck!!! I remember being SO overly stimulated by that encounter that I actually went home and had to lie down. Carole King said hello to me. Carole King wished me luck! Carol King LOVES me!!!

So with that sadly misguided confidence, I crossed the street and zeroed right in on her and her beautiful little unsuspecting, vulnerable, innocent grandchildren.

I'm sure she (like many celebrities of her caliber) is used to being approached by inappropriately overzealous strangers. I said "HI" to her like she was my long-lost friend. Like I knew her. Like she knew me. She had a look of dubious curiosity, but nonetheless she remained tentatively gracious and open.

And then, I offered jelly beans to her grandchildren. Yes. I was a stranger offering candy to children. If there's ONE lesson all children are taught, it's NEVER TAKE CANDY FROM A STRANGER.

At that moment I learned Carole King is not only a world-class singer-songwriter, she is also an Olympic sprinter with epic strength and agility! She gathered those kids, turned them 180 degrees, and PUFF. They were GONE. It was as if they had vaporized.

And there I stood, bag in hand, CHASTISING MY-SELF. HOW could I have been so stupid? What was I thinking? Dear God, Carole King HATES ME!

I have thought of that incident many times over the years, always with hideous feelings of embarrassment and remorse. That memory has kept me awake at night. I can't even eat jelly beans anymore! Fortunately, this story does not end here, and life has a funny way of healing wounds, dulling pain, forgiving mistakes.

In recent years I got to meet Robbie Kondor. He's a brilliant musician, and coincidentally, HE'S THE FATHER OF THOSE TWO UNSUSPECTING CHILDREN to whom I innocently offered candy so long ago.

They have grown up to become fine, upstanding citizens of the world! Robbie ASSURES ME that they were not scarred for life because of my unsolicited advances.

He PROMISES ME they were not traumatized. In fact, he says they don't even remember the incident. I'll bet Carole King remembers it. I know I remember it.

—JULIE GOLD

★

I sing and play accordion in a two-time Grammy-nominated family music rock band called Brady Rymer and the Little Band That Could. We've played all over the country and have met such wonderful people. In June 2016, we were doing a live radio concert at SiriusXM in New York City called "Kids Place Live" hosted by a woman in DC named Mindy Thomas. About halfway into our show Brady says,

"Mindy, you can't see this because you're in DC, but Steven Tyler of Aerosmith is waving at us through the glass. Mindy? I think he's coming in!" The door flies open and in walks Steven in all of his rock-and-roll glory. I'm thinking to myself, "Oh my God, he's walking towards me." He gets close and says, "My dad used to play the accordion!" Brady says, "Steven, this is a kids show we are doing and we would love it if you'd sing with us." Before I knew it, he got on my microphone with me and joined us in a song. At the end of the song he whispered in my ear one of the following things: "I love you," "I want you," or "You have a piece of kale in your teeth." He shook Brady's hand, our mandolin player's—Liz Queler—hand and turned around to look at us and said, "Wow, thank you so much. Wow." Wow indeed. He was genuine and beautiful and as sweet as could be.

—CLAUDIA GLASER-MUSSEN

NINE

INCREDIBLE INJECTIBLES

Finding the Line in the Celebrity Sand

★

On a recent night out with a group of friends, there was much talk about what everyone does to their faces. I had to be honest, my face really didn't bother me that much.

"That's because when you look in the mirror you make a Botox face," my friend Ann said. Of course, in the mirror I raise my eyebrows and don't smile. If only I could remember to do that in the world. Ann happens to be very beautiful and natural-looking and she spends most of her days with dogs and horses. So how did she end up trying out Botox?

"I had gone to the Emmys with Denis [her husband, the actor Denis Leary], and the next day I looked at photos of the event online. People were commenting on all of these celebrity websites about how noble it was for Denis to still be with his 'old wife.'" She said, "I was insulted and he was buoyed!" The next day she went out and got a little Botox in her frown lines.

Ann is the wife of a big celebrity, but she's also a bestselling author, which means that every couple of years she's in the public eye . . . as I am. It sometimes involves photo shoots with plenty of chances for your face to get fixed in the "post" process. I've even had a photo editor lighten my dark roots before a picture ran in a paper. Or maybe a TV appearance with more makeup tricks than Stan Winston, or reading in front of a bunch of people who don't expect you to be flawless. As far as my public goes (three dogs on my couch), my face could have an extra eye and no one would notice or care. Not so with celebrities, and in recent years what actors, musical performers, and even politicians (hello, Joe Biden hair plugs) have to do to their faces and bodies to maintain any sort of career staying power has come to the forefront of discussions, next to issues like wage inequality.

Sometimes something will remind me of an actor or actress I haven't seen in a while and I'll Google them. If the first image that comes up is not a mug shot, I assume they've aged out of roles. Ironically, one of my favorite movies from the 1990s was about a plastic surgeon, *Doc Hollywood*. I saw it in a movie theater when it was released in 1991, and it hit me in the sweet spot. I loved the story: a cocky young doctor named Ben Stone (Michael J. Fox) is driving to Hollywood in pursuit of a high-paying career as a plastic surgeon to the rich and famous. En route he crashes his car on a small-town judge's property in South Carolina and incurs a community-service fine, to be served out at the local hospital assisting the aged town doctor, Dr. Hogue (Barnard Hughes). Ben is soon tempted to stay by a pretty, sassy ambulance driver, Lou (Julie Warner), and there's a pet pig. I loved the characters, I loved the character of the town, and that pig. It was a cozy, perfect movie, one that I happily bought on DVD, as it was guaranteed to reduce the day's stress while I ate my dinner with my dog Otto.

After the success of *Doc Hollywood*, its female lead, Julie Warner, appeared in *Mr. Saturday Night* in 1992 and *Tommy Boy* in 1995, and she developed absolute star power. But in recent years I hadn't seen her as much, and I wondered what had happened. Her story is an object lesson in the persona an actor creates.

We spoke in 2015 and she filled me in on where she'd been and how she started. "I came out to Los Angeles in '87 at age twenty-two. I did all the things then that I thought I was supposed to do. I was in a great acting class with an amazing teacher who coached me on every movie script. He gave me so much confidence. So much of the momentum when you make it is confidence. And then, suddenly, I got *Doc Hollywood*, which I never in a million years thought I would get. I went in with that attitude of they're never going to hire me, but I knew I had the confidence and the part was in my wheelhouse. I had no nerves about the actual audition and as the process went on and they kept calling me back. All of the sudden I was in a room with Michael J. Fox reading a script to see if he likes me. I thought, 'Wow, this is getting real.'

"And that was the moment. That part changed my entire

life, and though I didn't get an enormous amount of money, for me at the time it was more money than I had ever seen and they treated me like a star and my name was above the title and suddenly I'm thrust into this world of getting invited to A-list parties.

"A week after *Doc Hollywood* opened, it was number two at the box office, and I got the part in *Mr. Saturday Night*. I shot that movie for five or six months. It took a long time for that movie. There were huge expectations because it was Billy Crystal's big movie after *City Slickers* and he was starring, directing, and writing."

Mr. Saturday Night did not do well at the box office.

"When it came out, that also changed my life. My agent at CAA at the time, who was Jewish, said, 'Well, now you've been outed as a Jewish actress.' I said, what does that mean? He said, 'It pains me to say this, but now people know you're Jewish.'"

I gasp listening to her. This was in 1993, not 1933.

"He said, 'The people who saw you as the cute Southern girl in *Doc Hollywood* are now going to think when you walk into the room that you remind them of their daughter or sister or wife. And nobody wants that.'

"It was unreal. I couldn't believe what I was hearing. I was so blown away. He just said you have to accept that your options are going to be limited in a certain way. And I thought, thanks for the heads-up."

Options are always limited for actors. Not everyone is right for every part. Actors are restricted by their physical appearance, age, experience, and the style of the time, but the idea of being limited by their religion is very unsettling to me.

She continues, "When I went in for *Tommy Boy*, they wanted

me to play the part but I had to go in twice, because the second time they wanted me to go in with my naturally curly hair blow-dried straight, because they wanted to see if I could look more Midwestern and less Jewish or ethnic. I'm not a particularly Semitic-looking person . . ." (No kidding.) "Again, everything has changed," she adds. "Now there are Jewish actresses all over the place—Natalie Portman, Rachel Weisz . . . Back then it was only Winona Ryder.

"It's been weird with that, and being against the status quo as an offbeat beauty was at a certain time totally fine. Debra Winger is Jewish and has an amazing career, but would she have one now? That's a question. When you look at her when she was young, she had a great body and was beautiful, but she was offbeat and didn't look like a model. When I started, actors looked more like models. I'm a character actress. I want different types of roles. The straight-up ingénue or the bland-girl part or the pretty-girl part is not usually that well written, and if it is well written, you're not doing it—Julia Roberts is doing it."

That in itself can make it more difficult to be a big celebrity.

Julie agrees. "That has been a really interesting sidebar to my career frustration: looks. And now there's also age. It doesn't matter what people say—'You don't look like you've aged at all' or 'You look amazing'—people know how old you are. I've never lied about my age. It's on my IMDb page and you can't change it. I remember when IMDb first appeared. I was working on *Family Law* with the late, great Dixie Carter, and she was like, 'Julie! You have to do something about this. My birthday is on the computer! You and your smart friends must know how to fix that!' She said it was very unladylike, a huge invasion of her privacy, and if she wanted to lie about her age, that was her right."

We talk about how crazy ageism is in every field, but much more so in the world of celebrity. As a woman who lives on this earth, I'm aware that there are a few "imbalances" in how men and women are treated and seen. For example, men get paid more than women for doing the same job. Now take that notion to Hollywood and watch your head explode.

In 2002 Doris Roberts, the legendary actress who died in 2012 at the age of ninety (she was still working!) with a career that spanned fifty years, most famously as Marie Barone on *Everybody Loves Raymond*, testified before the Senate Special Committee on Aging in Media and Marketing. Roberts said, "My profession, the entertainment business, is one of the worst perpetrators of this bigotry, particularly when it comes to women . . . When a sixty-year-old actor portrays a married man, his wife is likely to be young enough to be his daughter. Think of Michael Douglas paired with Gwyneth Paltrow in the remake of *Dial M for Murder* or Sean Connery married to Catherine Zeta-Jones."

Aging isn't easy for anyone. Recently I had one of those horrible colds that make you wish there was a worse word for it than *cold*. Aside from my usual red nose, my eyelids were swollen— Tippi the Turtle eyes. Between bouts of self-pity and more self-pity, it occurred to me that those eyelids might actually be a permanent addition to my future. I had just turned fifty (or as I refer to it, "fiddy"). I started searching "eyelid lifts" and realized that unless they permitted Kickstarters for vanity surgery, I was shit out of luck: youth does not come cheap.

I tucked it in the back of my mind, where it stayed until a

few weeks later, when all my social media feeds erupted in a frenzy over Renée Zellweger's new face. (I had not realized this, but at the time she had been out of the public eye for four years.) I used to mock celebrities who had excessive plastic surgery (OK, I still do, but never publicly! And never on a Sunday!), but in the past couple of years I've had my turtle eyes opened. When Kim Novak was mocked for how she looked at the Oscars in 2014 and admitted how hurt she had been by all the criticism and that she'd been terrified about appearing in public for the first time in years (she was EIGHTY-ONE YEARS OLD at the time, people) and that she just wanted to look her best, my heart broke for her.

Then right after the controversy about Kim Novak, Frances McDormand was quoted in the *New York Times* about celebrities getting plastic surgery. "Something happened culturally: No one is supposed to age past 45—sartorially, cosmetically, attitudinally," said McDormand, who has been married to director Joel Coen for more than thirty years. "Everybody dresses like a teenager. Everybody dyes their hair. Everybody is concerned about a smooth face."

I loved her for saying it, but let's call a spade a spade: Frances McDormand and Renée Zellweger are two totally different Oscar-winning celebrities with two totally different kinds of careers. Frances was never the girl in *Jerry Maguire*. Renée was not Marge in *Fargo*. While these talented women are famous and recognizable, they're famous in different ways and they look different because of it.

It's not news that men, from actors to politicians, don't live under the same kind of scrutiny that women do. They are allowed to age and have gray hair, and their appearance doesn't have as much of an impact on their careers (beyond the obvious of someone like Harrison Ford no longer being able to hang from a Nazi tank in the deserts of the Middle East). That just ain't so for the gals. One of my favorite Tina Fey quotes from her book *Bossypants* is "I know older men in comedy who can barely feed and clean themselves, and they still work. The women, though, they're all 'crazy.' I have a suspicion—and hear me out, because this is a rough one—that the definition of 'crazy' in show business is a woman who keeps talking even after no one wants to fuck her anymore."

Doris Roberts was less a victim of ageism: Because she was definitively a character actress, it was not only OK but also necessary for her to look like someone's mother or grandmother and not someone "you wanted to fuck." She also didn't come of age in the extreme-plastic-surgery era. We now have story after story of plastic surgery nightmares: Heidi Montag with her ten plastic surgeries in one day and then a further breast enlargement to an F cup (and then regret, and a reduction back to a C); Jennifer Grey, whose nose job stopped her career; Olivia Goldsmith, the author of *The First Wives Club*, who died having a tummy tuck. And though those are the extremes, the real problem is the actresses who don't seem to know when to stop. And there are plenty of men, too. Mickey Rourke claims the excessive plastic surgery he had done to his face was an answer to years of boxing, but people who boxed with him said he was never hit in the face, so who knows? How about Kenny Rogers's eyes? And have you seen Burt Reynolds? And Keith Richards! (Oh, wait, he hasn't had plastic surgery. Never mind.)

It wasn't that there were no adjustments in the old days. Rita Hayworth famously had her hairline electrolyzed, Marilyn Monroe had a nose job and her jaw reshaped. Jean Harlow's hair was bleached so much that it nearly fell out. But all those changes pale in comparison with the current crop of endless injectibles that celebrities are using to try to stop time. It's a real problem when people whose job is to express their emotions through their faces can't move them.

The actress Amanda Peet wrote in the web magazine *Lenny Letter* about her refusal to get fillers, mainly because she was scared. "I'm afraid one visit to a cosmetic dermatologist would be my gateway drug. I'd go in for a tiny, circumscribed lift and come out looking like a blowfish. Or someone whose face is permanently pressed up against a glass window. Or like I'm standing in the jet stream of a 747. What's the point of doing it if everyone can tell? I want the thing that makes me look younger, not the thing that makes me look like I did the thing."

She, like Julie Warner, is not willing to play this kind of celebrity roulette. For the women of her—my—generation, who grew up in the "Free to Be You and Me" era, it always seemed like a no-brainer. Be who you are, you can cry if you want to, even if you're a boy. Run fast if you're a girl. Be different. Get older. As Julie puts it: "I've never lied about my age. I mean, what's the point anyway? People know how long you've been around. I'm still reading for parts in my forties. I'm pushing the envelope of forty, but I'm small and I do look young for my age." And that's genetics; Julie isn't a "user."

"People know who I am but they also want to check me out: 'How is she looking this week? How is her weight? Has she had any work done?' If you're a character actress, no one gives a crap. But honestly it's great that Kathy Najimy has lost weight, but she's Kathy Najimy and she gets these great parts—she's on *Veep*. The point is, character actresses work and nobody cares or checks out their butt." (The same goes for writers.)

That realization didn't come easy to Julie. "I used to work my ass off—literally—to be in perfect shape," she says. "This is the years after I had [her son] Jackson and I was thirty-two, so I had to work with a trainer and did ten million spin classes. I worked really hard and was on the Zone diet and did all that stuff. I came back and was in the best shape of my life and looked great when I was on *Family Law*. But I was in my mid-thirties and it was easier then.

"Being a professional athlete or an actor who is constantly trying to be at the peak of their physical fitness and maintain their perfect whatever—it gets harder as you get older. I realize now what I took for granted. Now I have gray hairs and have to deal with that."

But you can change your gray hairs in a couple of hours. Bodies are different. Julie says, "Once there was a thing on the internet about 'Julie Warner weight gain,' like a trending thing, and I almost died. Why would someone do that? I was convinced it was a mean person with a vendetta against me."

Such concern for putting forth the right image has been one of the hallmarks of celebrity for decades. Deanna Durbin, who was a huge movie star and singer in the 1930s and '40s, famously declared when she retired from show business in 1949, "I hated being in a goldfish bowl." At the time she was twenty-nine years old.

"When my first marriage failed, everyone said that I could never divorce. It would ruin the *'image,'*" Durbin told Robert Shipman in *Films and Filming* magazine in 1983. "How could anybody really think that I was going to spend the rest of my life with a man I found I didn't love, just for the sake of an *'image'*?" She turned her back on her celebrity, marrying twice more, ultimately to the director Charles David, with whom she moved to France and lived in a farmhouse. Deanna spent her days cooking and cleaning and raising her family.

Julie Warner is aware of the hit-and-miss of the whole business. "Between the time *Family Law* ended and I got divorced—from my mid-thirties to my early forties—I filmed a bunch of pilots that didn't go. I could feel the window closing. When you've been successful for twenty-plus years and done really well—to me it was never about being the celebrity. There are actors and actresses who care a great deal about being celebrities. That was never my thing. I remember my agent having conversations with me about going to more parties and networking more. I just didn't want that."

Keeping yourself in the public eye, both within the world you work and to the larger masses, is one of the keys to maintaining celebrity. "Ninety percent of this business is staying power," Julie says. "You have to hang in there. You watch athletes and they know they have a time limit. There are no fifty-year-old quarterbacks. There are no fifty-year-olds in the NBA. The problem for actors is there really is no afterlife."

And the lack of an afterlife for celebrities is even worse.

"I look at our celebrities now and I wonder, who is a celebrity? I don't know if I would have pursued a career in acting if I had known there would be Kardashians or shows not based on talent. There's a whole generation of people who don't know the movies I was in. Now I have to ask myself, are you going to give up or plow ahead and say there's a second act for you and it's going to be better than the first and you're grown up now and you're going to do it? Keep going and fight the pain . . . stop comparing yourself and stop all the voices and say this is your path."

In 2016, Jennifer Aniston wrote a brilliant (and that's just not my opinion, several fellow celebrities tweeted it) response to all of the ridiculous speculation about her—she said, "For the record, I am *not* pregnant. What I am is *fed up.*" She went on to say, "The objectification and scrutiny we put women through is absurd and disturbing. The way I am portrayed by the media is simply a reflection of how we see and portray women in general, measured against some warped standard of beauty. Sometimes cultural standards just need a different perspective so we can see them for what they really are—a collective acceptance . . . a subconscious agreement. We are in charge of our agreement. Little girls everywhere are absorbing our agreement, passive or otherwise. And it begins early. The message that girls are not pretty unless they're incredibly thin, that they're not worthy of our attention unless they look like a supermodel or an actress on the cover of a magazine is something we're all willingly buying into. This conditioning is something girls then carry into womanhood. We use celebrity 'news' to perpetuate this dehumanizing view of females, focused solely on one's physical appearance, which tabloids turn into a sporting event of speculation. Is she pregnant? Is she eating too much? Has she let herself go? Is her marriage on the rocks because the camera detects some physical 'imperfection'?

"I used to tell myself that tabloids were like comic books, not to be taken seriously, just a soap opera for people to follow when they need a distraction. But I really can't tell myself that anymore because the reality is the stalking and objectification I've experienced first-hand, going on decades now, reflects the warped way we calculate a woman's worth."

What Jennifer wrote was perfect, and the more people perpetuate her ideas, the better it will be for all of us. It's extremely difficult to grow old as a normal woman, but doing it in front of the paparazzi is like being on trial, even though people are looking better and better at older ages then they did before, the scrutiny is maddening. Two of my life idols are Cher and Madonna.

Cher turned seventy in 2016 and tweeted that for her birthday she was going to "eat cake and cry." When a fan tweeted her a photo of her young self and asked when it was taken, she responded, "Dinosaurs were still roaming the earth." She's funny about herself, and people love her.

Madonna, who turned fifty-eight in 2016, seems to inspire more indignation. There is a lot of "how dare she?" responses to her continuing to be out there (and I mean *out there*: she is not shy about continuing to dress and act provocatively). After the 2016 Met Gala, where she wore an outfit in which she had just sheer black lace covering her butt, she was soundly criticized. She released a statement that read, "My dress at the Met Ball was a political statement as well as a fashion statement. The fact that people actually believe a woman is not allowed to express her sexuality and be adventurous past a certain age is proof that we still live in an age-ist and sexist society. I have never thought in a limited way and I'm not going to start. We cannot effect change unless we are willing to take risks by being fearless and by taking the road less traveled by. That's how we change history. If you have a problem with the way I dress, it is simply a reflection of your prejudice. I'm not afraid to pave the way for all the girls behind me!! As Nina Simone once said, the definition of freedom is being fearless. I remain Unapologetic and a Rebel."

It has not escaped my irony meter that Sean Connery was fifty-nine when *People* magazine crowned him the "Sexiest Man Alive."

I firmly believe that if anyone can change the way celebrities are allowed to age, it's Madge. She's rebuffed the haters (and there have been many) for more than thirty years, and she shows no signs of stopping. That may be the smartest age-defying practice of all.

Intermission 9

In 1989 or 1990, during my first year in New York, I was standing by myself up in the balcony at some old music venue in Midtown Manhattan. I can't remember which band was playing. As I stood at the railing, looking down at the crowd and the stage, drinking my vodka on the rocks, I sensed someone near me, standing just behind me, to my right. I distinctly remember fighting the urge to turn around to see who it was, because I knew it was someone famous. Finally I snuck a glance and beheld Mick Jagger. It was just me and him up in the balcony, looking down together. My glance was a fast flick, just long enough to take in how diminutive and elegant he was, how beautifully he held himself, like a dancer, and how totally . . . fucking . . . cool Mick Jagger was in person. A big dude with folded arms stood just outside the doorway to the balcony, behind us: I assumed he was Mick's bodyguard. So Mick and I had a moment together, whether he liked it or not. Me: drunk, twenty-seven, naïve, awestruck, and intensely thrilled and shocked to see him there. Mick: quiet, self-contained, not looking back at me but fully aware that I'd seen him, no doubt wearily waiting for me to blurt out something fawning and wreck the moment. Reader, I did not. I turned my attention back to my drink and my thoughts and the stage. When I next turned to look, he was gone.

—KATE CHRISTENSEN

One lovely summer Friday night in 2008 in the West Village, my now wife, Jackie, and I were walking home from dinner at a local restaurant. Of course, we had Mitzi in tow, in her bag. We were half a block up 12th Street, heading to Greenwich Street, when I saw three African American men standing on the corner. The man in the center was wearing a baseball uniform, a large gold pendant hanging from a thick chain, and a red baseball cap turned sideways. The other two men were obviously bodyguards (their size said it all). I said to Jackie, "Come with me," and crossed the street to approach the corner. She said nothing to me, but I knew exactly who this was, because I had seen P. Diddy on some kind of talk show the day before, announcing his new reality show that would ultimately choose an assistant for P. Diddy. He was wearing that same outfit, so that's how I knew who was standing there . . . just the three of them. No one else.

So, these two middle-aged white women saunter right on over, and I say to Diddy, "Hey, what're you doing in my hood?" Is there is anything more pathetic than a middle-age Jewish white chick desperately trying to be so rap-artist cool? Diddy replied, "Just chillin'," making me feel like I really was a member of his tribe. He held out his hand to shake mine, and I said, "I'm Gail, this is Jackie, and this is Mitzi!" He couldn't have cooed more over Mitzi (the way to my heart, for sure). We stood and chatted for what seemed like an eternity, but was probably forty-five seconds, me talking about his clothing line and who knows what else. He was so patient and kind. I said my good-bye, wished him well, and off we went.

—GAIL DOSIK

★

Snow Patrol was one of the first bands I met when I started on KNRK in 2004. They'd never been to America before, and they were shy, nervous, and incredibly gracious guys. Plus, they were adorable and Irish. As we were the station that premiered them in the States, they also did exclusive events with us during their early tours. They played small sessions for contest winners that I would always host, and I introduced them at every live show they played for us during my five years there. When my son Jack was seven, I brought him to one such live session, and afterwards he got to meet the band. He and Gary Lightbody discussed the Beatles. Gary took to him immediately because his own father's name is Jack. I have a very sweet photo of them together.

The day of the show, where I got a shout-out, Gary was in the studio with me. We talked about how on their previous visit he had mentioned to me how he was such a big fan of the Foo Fighters, and Snow Patrol was about to play their biggest show yet in LA, where the Foos live. Of course I'd immediately emailed the Foo's tour manager to see if he could get Dave Grohl to that show. I told him I just knew Snow Patrol was going to be a huge band and how much Gary admired Dave. He did indeed go, and they got to meet. Gary was so man-crushing on Dave that he said on the air, "Dave Grohl shouldn't just be president of America—he should be president of the world!"

—TARA DUBLIN

TEN

REALITY BITES

★

When you speak to people about the nature of celebrity, there's a point in the conversation when they get uncomfortable or agitated and you know what they're going to say: "What about the Kardashians?" Though the family is a gazillion-dollar enterprise, I don't meet a lot of people who feel a fondness for them. A large sector of the population bristles at reality TV celebrities, and just as some people refer to pornography or embezzlement but claim not to participate in it, these non-reality fans take pride in not knowing anything about reality celebrities.

Yet millions of people seem to want to know where these reality stars came from. I am just as uncertain as the rest of the world is, but I like to think of them in terms of Greek mythology. Zeus heard that the goddess Metis's firstborn was going to overthrow him, so he swallowed her and her unborn child. Zeus then developed an unbearable headache, which made him wail in pain so loudly that it could be heard throughout the universe. The other gods immediately realized what needed to be done. They would have to take a wedge and split Zeus's skull open. (Note to self: don't get a headache in ancient Greece.)

Move that metaphor into the world of today—and boom: From the collective migraine of television executives everywhere spring the stars of reality TV: Richard Hatch. Honey Boo Boo. Lauren Conrad. Spencer Pratt and Heidi Montag. The Situation and Snooki. Omarosa. Kate Gosselin. Bethenny Frankel. Teresa Giudice. And of course Kris, Khloé, Kourtney, Kendall, Kylie, and Kim Kardashian (and Caitlyn Jenner).

What's important to remember is that there has always been reality TV, even before it was called that. Way back in the 1960s there was *Candid Camera*, which was a forerunner of sorts—a show that put normal people in extraordinary circumstances and filmed their reactions, for the humor in it. And in the 1970s PBS aired the twelve-episode documentary series *An American Family* about the Loud family of Santa Barbara, California, which was the first sort of "invisible" camera in the home.

But reality television didn't explode till a couple of decades later. We had a program inspired by *An American Family* in MTV's *The Real World* in 1992, and then the half-game-show, half-reality-show *Survivor* debuted in 2000. Since then and little by little, nonscripted television has taken over the airwaves, much to the crushing horror of the people whose job it was to create scripted TV shows.

Much about reality TV has been debated since. How did it

become so popular, so ubiquitous? Was there a realignment of the universe that made people suddenly want to see inside strangers' homes or be publicly humiliated on camera? Did it have something to do with Al Gore's invention of the internet? And perhaps the most complicated question of all: Does everybody today want to be a celebrity?

The rise of reality television also raises a question about a new kind of celebrity: What is the difference between a traditional celebrity and a reality TV celebrity? All singers, actors, dancers, athletes, and politicians have something that appeals to us; a physical talent or training, a certain gift or ability. Reality TV celebrities seem to have an overarching desire to be famous at any cost. And more and more we seem to be willing to accept that—and them. Some of these reality stars are talented. Some of them are beautiful. Some of them are wily. Some of them are just appalling. And some are no different than you or I.

The idea of reality celebrities is that the camera is catching, and we are watching, "average" people being themselves. Of course there is no way that the introduction of a camera doesn't change how a person behaves, so they are as much themselves as Robert De Niro was himself in *Taxi Driver*. They are playing a part in whatever drama, competition, or situation the television show frames around them.

And many of them are far from average. We may feel we know them because they are "regular" people, but the characters they are playing are themselves, at least theoretically. We may like them or hate them, look up to them or look down our noses at them. But they are supposed to be *real*: they're supposed to be like us. Whether they're running down a beach in an immunity challenge or giving a rose to the bachelor of their choice, we are watching them deal with the tests life throws at them.

In all honesty, I am not a big fan of reality TV. I've watched episodes of *American Idol, The Osbournes,* and *The Littlest Groom* (because I'd just had a baby and I was mentally deficient). Actually I watched most of *American Idol* before I had a kid. I remember when I was pregnant and had to get up every hour to pee, I would stop by my phone and redial votes for my favorite *American Idol* contestants (Charles Grigsby, George Huff, Ruben Studdard). But once my daughter was born, I had more important things to worry about than padding some unknown singer's votes.

Though many people see reality television as a guilty escapist pleasure, reality shows make me tense. I don't enjoy confrontation, and I don't like watching people being sneaky or subversive or immoral. I don't mind seeing it in a movie or play, because I know it's not real. I know that Michael Douglas isn't really plotting Gwyneth Paltrow's death; he's just *pretending.* When the director says "cut," they'll all have a big laugh! But reality players are (at least in theory) doing real things to real people, often for unsavory reasons. The mother on *Toddlers and Tiaras,* for example, *is* actually doping up her six-year-old with "go-go juice," a mixture of Red Bull and Mountain Dew, to keep her daughter alert. And a parent rewards her chubby *Child Genius* contestant with candy for correctly answering a question.

Though my aunt Mattie and I have always had a like-minded view of the world, and I look to her for guidance and answers to questions about life, our preferred programming is where we part company. She loves reality shows; I don't. I tried to explore them to give me some background for this book, but it wasn't long before I realized that it wasn't working. I am not the audience for these shows. If you are, you would not want to hear my smug takedown of these programs.

To get a clearer sense of the appeal of reality TV shows, I turned to people who enjoy these programs, including that paragon of culture, Aunt Mattie.

At a recent gathering of my friends—all women—almost everyone confessed to loving *The Real Housewives* franchise while only a few waved away the notion that they'd ever be watching anything other than *Downton Abbey*.

One friend, Diana, loves the *Real Housewives*. She is a novelist and an amateur sleuth. (She has actually uncovered a crime and evidence and brought it to the authorities.) Her personal life is fairly quiet and drama-free, so I was surprised when she admitted that she liked these shows that are nothing but drama. She says of her reasoning for watching the *Real Housewives* programs, "No matter how lazy, shallow, or narcissistic I might believe myself to be, in comparison to any of the housewives, I am, and most women I know are, like Mother Teresa. Suddenly I'm the best wife and mother in the world. I mean, these women would eat their young for screen time."

But it's more than that, Diana says: "It also has to do with my fascination with female behavior. The way that women align themselves with certain women and against others. The New Jersey and Atlanta housewives are the two I like least, because those have husbands as major players, and the men are just not as interesting. The New Jersey housewives have more drama among the men than the women. They are also the stupidest of all the housewives groups."

Aunt Mattie remembers watching Teresa Giudice, one of the New Jersey housewives, buying thousands of dollars of furniture with cash and thinking, "Doesn't she know the IRS has TVs?" She turned out to be right: Teresa and her husband, Joe, pleaded guilty to tax fraud and both went to jail (though not at the same time). More drama for their franchise (including T-shirts that read "FREE TRE").

I ask Diana why she thinks these housewives are willing to behave the way they do on TV. Her theory is that the participants have access to alcohol all the time, which reduces their inhibitions and screws with their judgment. "You know, they get really horny and then they act on it. That's when the drama happens." A little chardonnay can be a dangerous thing.

Diana also raises an interesting point about these programs regarding children. "I think there should be a law forbidding people from putting their children on these reality shows, though," she says. "The kids are too young to consent. I remember on the New York housewives, one of them, Jill Zarin, outed her daughter for going to a fat camp. I mean she used some euphemism, but the kid went to one of those fancy private schools on the Upper East Side, mean-girl central, and here is her mother blabbing about her daughter doing the most embarrassing thing you could imagine."

Part of the appeal of shows like this, Diana argues, is the

water-cooler aspect to them. "My sister and I text throughout the Beverly Hills and New York housewives episodes. We like to make fun of them."

Yet she admits there is also an aspect of watching these shows that makes her hate herself: "It's like watching porn, you know?" It may make you feel bad about yourself, but people keep watching.

Another friend said her interest in reality TV is not unlike her interest in strangers' medicine cabinets. "If I look in there, I can get a quick and accurate psychological profile," she explains. "People's medications (which no one thinks to lock), insecurities ('age-defying' lotions, mouthwash, whitening toothpaste, hair-growth capsules). Rich people always have perfume in their medicine cabinets, because they don't really give a crap if the heat from the bathroom spoils it—they can just buy another! [Helpful tip from someone who isn't rich: We keep our perfume in the refrigerator.] So there's an economic reading—is there Chanel face cream, which costs hundreds of dollars, even though dermatologists tell you CeraVe works just as well for ten bucks? Then they have money they can toss into the nearby toilet. Or some people look neat outwardly, but their brush hasn't been cleaned in two years and looks like a hamster. It's all just sort of telling."

Reality shows are the medicine cabinets of TV. Also these shows are a bit like soft-core porn. They're titillating but you don't need to hide them in a plain brown wrapper. They're acceptable if embarrassing.

Reality programming has two general categories: the contest shows and the exploration shows. The contest shows like *Survivor* and *The Bachelor* and *The Voice* are fairly straightforward:

the goal is to win something—money, "love," a record deal, or just staying on a TV show longer. The people on these shows also have talents: singing, designing clothes, modeling, or physical prowess.

The ones that simply involve exploring a segment of the population's lives are different. The only talent the people on those shows have is a colossal lack of shame.

For deeper insight into the impact of reality television, though, I turned to my secret weapon: Aunt Mattie, who not only collects all kinds of celebrity information but also watches a lot of television. Of course *The Housewives*, but also (past and present) *Vanderpump Rules, Shahs of Sunset, Southern Charm, Newlyweds: The First Year, Married at First Sight, Mob Wives, Total Divas, Survivor, Love & Hip Hop, The Osbournes*, and *Keeping Up with the Kardashians*. Her reality show tastes run the gamut.

Part of their fun for Aunt Mattie is that she likes talking about them with people—by tweeting and posting her thoughts on message boards. Live-tweeting a lot of these shows is a hugely popular pastime—*The Bachelor* and *The Bachelorette* generate millions of tweets over the course of a season. While there's no public data on the tone of these tweets, from what I've been able to find, many of the tweets about the shows are mocking the contestants. They're like yelling at your favorite baseball player for striking out or sitting in on the parliamentary debates in a Victorian novel and listening to the politicians make fun of one another and their ideas.

Mattie prefers the exploration shows to the contest shows. And she has very specific and well-considered opinions about reality television and the celebrity that springs from it.

"My friends and family always say to me, 'Mattie, you're so smart and beautiful. Why do you watch such dumb TV?'" (She's right about this—we do.)

"I think it's because I've always loved conflict," she says. "I like to be sitting next to people in a restaurant who are having a fight. I remember renting a house in the Hamptons when I was first married and the room next to ours held a couple whose wife used their private time to criticize her husband's behavior while carefully removing whatever backbone he had shown early in the marriage. Incidentally, this is when I found out that a glass reversed and pressed against the wall truly is effective as a microphone. That, in a nutshell, is reality TV to me. It's like being at the next table with people who are spilling their guts for you to enjoy."

I decide to watch some of these reality shows with Mattie, so one afternoon I sit down with her in the bedroom of her Manhattan apartment. Two La-Z-Boy chairs—one for Mattie and her Boston terrier, Raymond, the other for me and my razor-sharp wit—face a big flat-screen TV. Between us is a TV table with some licorice and pretzels.

First up on the big small screen is *Love & Hip-Hop: Hollywood*. I recognize it from someone else's treadmill monitor at the gym. It is a show about fledgling hip-hop artists and the gals who love them.

Mattie explains, "I was first attracted to this show because it included Ray J, the gentleman who was the second banana"—

she winks—"in the sex tape that made Kim Kardashian famous. Ray J is one of the few people on these shows who are actually successful in show business. That doesn't stop the rest of them from spending time in studios, becoming managers, and talking about their 'brand.'" While this makes me laugh, I don't get how she stays with the show for the full episode.

"What draws me to *Love and Hip-Hop* is the relationships. This show is filled with absolutely gorgeous women who have multiple children with mediocre-looking guys who rarely support those children. Once I watched an episode of *Love and Hip-Hop: Hollywood* where a guy, one of the few who was married, was telling his wife that before he leaves for prison, he wanted to get all of his baby mamas together so they can be a comfort to each other while he's away."

"I can see why you like it," I say.

"If you're going to be Judgy McJudgerson, I'm not going to help you with your book," she replies.

"Continue," I say.

"Every minor slight among the women results in a vicious brawl that includes scratching and hair pulling. They become physical at anything that even suggests disrespect. I saw an episode where one woman, a rap manager, beat up another rap manager for bringing to a show someone that she 'should have known' the first woman didn't like. I just hope that none of my friends brings Patty Fitzimmons to any party I'm at, since Patty called me fat in 1952, or it'll be lights out for that friend."

While the fights on the *Love & Hip-Hop* shows are pretty good, they're nothing compared to what we watch next, *Mob Wives*.

. . .

*M*ob *Wives* is totally a Mattie show. It's like *Goodfellas*, only it's real and about women who've had lots of plastic surgery. When I was young I dated a mobster/bank robber, and Mattie was the only one who liked hanging out with him. (Though she always clutched her purse in his presence.)

"It is my kind of show," she agrees. "These women are not totally foreign to me. I grew up in the Bronx, but they are the women I knew cubed. This show is a symphony. Every time one of these women comes on the screen, their mob connections are written at the bottom. They are complete with length of prison stay, along with their names, including their nicknames. I sometimes wonder why a mob-connected woman would bother naming her son Anthony when everyone will only be calling him 'the Nose.'"

She has a point.

"These women can fight, and the threats of what they're going to do to their victims is poetry to my ears, from smashing them to infinity to making them ask permission to go to the bathroom.

"Another detail that makes these women special is that they sprinkle every sentence with at least four forms of the *F*-word. They use it as a noun, an adjective, an adverb, and a gerund—I know I've forgotten a few."

Still, there's a certain education in these shows. "It is clear that the worst thing you can be in Staten Island is a rat," Mattie says. "This is interesting since one of the stars of the show is

Karen Gravano, the daughter of Sammy 'the Bull' Gravano, whose 'ratting' put John Gotti, the Teflon Don, away."

But Mattie admits, "I guess all is forgiven since Victoria Gotti has appeared on the show, although I believe that was only to advise Big Ang not to speak to anyone you aren't related to."

I will admit the show is interesting, but after watching an episode I feel like I need to take a shower.

No need: we are going to the cleansing breezes of *Jersey Shore*.

Ah yes, *Jersey Shore*, the show that gave celebrity birth to Snooki and the Situation. I've seen it a couple of times, but watching with Mattie is like doing an audio tour at the Met. Now I'm really learning.

"This is a much younger group of Italian Americans, or as they call themselves, *guidos* and *guidettes*, on vacation," Mattie says. "On the first show they were all strangers to each other, but they became fast friends and bedmates. This show was on television several years ago, but I remember that the goal of every evening seemed to be to get fall-down drunk and 'shmush' someone. The boys described their lives in order of importance as Gym, Tan, Laundry."

Mattie also noted, "They did all the cooking using recipes that were clearly passed down by their grandmothers. Dinners in the Jersey Shore house were very much like the prison cooking scene from *Goodfellas*.

"One can't watch these shows without coming away with something, which is why now when I am speaking to more than one person I always use the familiar 'youse.'" Mattie the grammarian has spoken.

· 151 ·

She also watches what may currently be the ultimate reality show, *Keeping Up with the Kardashians,* but I thought it was unfair to have her pontificate on that one because their celebrity is so much larger than just the show.[1] So I let her get back to her DVR. Also, sitting in that La-Z-Boy for so long, I feel like I'm starting to get bedsores and I have an overwhelming desire to read some untranslated Dostoyevsky.

A lot of people wonder why the Kardashians are famous. They don't seem to have any specific talent for anything but being famous, taking selfies—not unlike their former and formerly more famous friend Paris Hilton did before them—and posting incessantly on social media.

Like many people, I first heard the name Kardashian in the mid-1990s during the O. J. Simpson trial. Robert Kardashian had been a friend of O.J.'s and became one of his defense lawyers. That in itself does not make for birthing a glamour clan. Mr. Kardashian married Kris and together the Kardashians had four children: Kourtney, Kim, Khloé, and K-Robert (the K is silent). Mr. Kardashian and Kris divorced, and Kris later married Olympic gold medalist Bruce Jenner and had two more daughters: Kendall and Kylie. The meshing of the Kardashian and Jenner clans seemed to be the spark that ignited Kardashistan.

Keeping Up with the Kardashians first aired in 2007, eons ago in reality years. At about the same time, Kim made a sex tape with rapper Ray J (future star of *Love & Hip Hop*). Though

---

1. She does want me to say that she finds the Kardashians very likable.

Kim claimed the tape was private and leaked without her knowledge, Ray J and others said its release was consensual and was a calculated step in her attempt to be famous like her former friend Paris Hilton. And though all the Kardashians seem to be equally talented (wink), Kim is the biggest celebrity. She dated a slew of famous men and married basketball player Kris Humphries in a magical ten-million-dollar wedding that they reportedly didn't have to pay a cent for because of the sale of photo rights and sponsorships. The marriage lasted only three months. As described by her next husband, Kanye West, when talking about something totally unrelated: "You know, it's like when my wife got a divorce, and I'm sorry, Kim, for mentioning this as an example but it's the best I have in front of me right now, she got a lot of backlash from it because her fans felt like somehow their dream was broken, because she's a dream girl and they're living vicariously through her in some way."

That was definitely how I felt. If Kim and Kris couldn't make it, what hope was there for the rest of us? Would she ever find another person with a *K* name to love? (I gave that part away already: yes, she found Kanye.) And those two have gone on to Kardashianate the world. They have their children North and Saint, Kanye seems to tweet eleven billion times a day, Bruce/ Caitlyn began a whole new life (complete with a new show), and the Kardashian fame train is showing no signs of slowing down.

Nor does the juggernaut of reality TV. As long as people are willing to open their medicine cabinets, there will be people who will want to peek in. And there seems to be no end to the people who want to be a celebrity in any way they can.

The downside of celebrity, we know, is that it fades. For reality celebrities, the sell-by date is even sooner, unless the reality celebrity moves on to something new that also catches the public's fancy, such as Bethenny Frankel and her Skinny Bitch cocktails. It doesn't always work, of course: A lot of people don't want to see reality celebrities reinvent themselves, especially if it involves respectability. (Except for Snooki, who in 2011, to the surprise of many in the publishing world and the despair of actual writers, became a *New York Times* bestselling novelist.)

And while some reality celebrities stay in our memories for good reasons—AIDS activist Pedro Zamora, from the second season of *The Real World*, who was HIV-positive and who helped raise awareness of the disease among younger people—the lesson for most reality stars is that they will only be in the spotlight until someone behind them is willing to do something more outrageous to catch the public's attention.

Intermission 10

Once my kids, nieces, and I were at Sweet Rose in Los Angeles, trying to cool off and also getting very good but overpriced ice cream. Six bucks a scoop. I mean, come on.

I was facing the door and have extremely excellent celebrity radar, so saw John Travolta walk in immediately.

My sister-in-law was visiting, and it is always fun to discreetly see huge superstars with out-of-town guests, so I leaned over and whispered to her.

All of the kids immediately demanded—loudly—to know what I had whispered.

I tried to ignore them because it was a small place and I didn't want to make a big deal of it. They wouldn't take no for an answer.

So I leaned over and said: "You know Grease? *That's Danny Zuko."*

And they shouted: "Oh my god, Danny Zuko!!!"

And my niece yelled: "That's the guy from Hairspray!!!"

And my daughter bellowed: "He doesn't look like Danny Zuko anymore!!! But maybe in his eyes!"

And I kept hissing: "Shhh! Stop! Be quiet! Don't make him uncomfortable!"

They quieted down a bit, so I thought maybe we had gotten away with not being assholes.

But then a few minutes later, after he got his six-dollar ice cream, he walked over and stopped quickly right in front of us and waved (literally) and said, "Bye-bye."

The kids' mouths dropped.

And I wanted to die.

—ALLISON WINN SCOTCH

★

It was about twenty years ago. My brother-in-law, Larry, was out in LA from New York, and he, my husband, Tom, some friends of Larry's who were also visiting, and I were going out to dinner.

Larry always got a great kick out of the idea of seeing celebrities, so he chose the Ivy by the Shore as the restaurant. Beautiful, overpriced, one of those places to "be seen."

We got there, we checked in, and they asked us to wait

until our table was ready. The waiting area was pretty crowded. There was no one recognizable, to Larry's dismay.

We didn't have to wait long to be called, and we all formed a path, single file, and followed the host towards the dining room.

I was bringing up the rear. Then, a very tall guy with hugely broad shoulders—granted, he was four inches from my face—wearing a black leather jacket, stepped right in my path, his back to me. Since it was crowded, there was no way to walk around him. So, I tapped very lightly on his back. I didn't want to be rude or startle him. No response. So I tapped just a very tiny bit harder. Nothing. Then a beat. Then he turns his head around—just his head—and looks at me. It's Gary Busey. And he says, "You'll get by. You'll get by." Then he turns his head back around and continues to talk with his friends!

I was more shocked than anything. What kind of behavior is this? It must be a new thing I'm not familiar with. Maybe something called "Acceptable Level of Rudeness."

A little time goes by, maybe a minute, which is way too long for anyone to do that, and he grants me a path. I'm shaking my head, and I walk in to find everyone, at the same time that Gary Busey is being shown to his table on the other side of the room. I looked at him as if to say, "What the hell is with you?" And he says, "Everything's going to be OK."

I sit down at our table, and Larry's friend says, "Hey, you know who that is? It's Gary Busey."

—CATHY LADMAN

ELEVEN

THE SORDID SPECTRUM OF CELEBRITY SCANDAL

★

Celebrities and scandals go together like prom night and a huge zit on your nose. It isn't *definitely* going to happen, but it's not surprising when it does.

It's important to define the different types of celebrity scandal. There are the uncomfortable wish-people-hadn't-found-out-about-this situations, such as the arrest tape of Reese Witherspoon and her husband in 2013. Jim Toth was pulled over on suspicion of driving while under the influence of alcohol and Reese was in the car, too, and she talked back to the cops when they were pulled over ("Do you know my name?"). It was a bad scene, but very quickly afterward Reese apologized. She issued a public statement that read in part: "I clearly had one drink too many and I am deeply embarrassed about the things I said. It was definitely a scary situation and I was frightened for my husband, but that is no excuse. I was disrespectful to the officer who was just doing his job. I have nothing but respect for the police and I'm very sorry for my behavior." She went on to publicly apologize for it again several times.

She and her husband did something unsafe and got caught, she overreacted, and she took responsibility for her actions. Her apology was honest and sincere, and in addition to being sorry about the act, she also regretted her rudeness. She handled it as well as any celebrity could.

Though I don't own a car and rarely drive, I believe being behind the wheel while you're not at your best happens to people—us non-celebrities—way more than it should. And to a certain extent we saw ourselves in Reese. Plus, she's Reese Witherspoon, not Gary Busey or Nick Nolte. We like Reese. She's normally on very good behavior. A year after the incident she was nominated for an Academy Award, a Golden Globe, a Screen Actors Guild Award, and a British Academy of Film and Television Award for best actress in the movie *Wild*, which she also produced. Clearly, she was forgiven.

Another type of scandal is the alleged extramarital affair. There have been countless stories of those over the years: Robin Williams and the nanny; Ethan Hawke and the nanny; Jude Law (who was only engaged to Sienna Miller) and the nanny; Shania Twain's husband, who had an affair with her secretary (and then Shania later married her secretary's ex-husband); Gwen Stefani and Blake Shelton (though allegedly Gavin Rossdale had been having affairs long before that, but he's not as famous); Brad and Angelina (and heaven knows who else). None of these events had any effect on the people's careers, but they were unfortunate PR situations, from which they mostly bounced back.

Yet that's not always the case. LeAnn Rimes and Eddie Cibrian, for example, were not blackballed by any means, but Leann's ex-husband, Dean Sheremet, told *Entertainment Tonight*, "The dumbest thing she ever did for her career was divorce me, because we were such a good team. The last hit song she had was when she was with me."

That may be true, but it was nothing compared with when Ingrid Bergman left her husband Petter Lindström in 1950 for Roberto Rossellini. This was an enormous scandal in postwar goody-goody America. American audiences that had been led to think of Bergman as the epitome of wholesome and beautiful womanhood were appalled when they learned of her affair with the Italian film director while she was married. Congress even discussed deporting her. Her Hollywood career came to a screeching halt, and it took several years of physical, literal and career exile before Bergman won Americans' hearts again, which she did with a comeback role in *Anastasia* in 1956, for which she won an Academy Award.

Of course, several years later, in 1959, when Eddie Fisher left America's sweetheart, Debbie Reynolds, for Elizabeth Taylor, the gossip was deafening but the professional fallout was minimal. Was it because Ingrid Bergman was a foreigner? Or not of the caliber of Elizabeth Taylor? Was it a different time? Who knows? Decades after the incident, I remember watching Carrie Fisher on *Late Night with David Letterman*, and when he asked her if she still harbored a grudge against Elizabeth Taylor, she said, "Well, I'm not going to buy her perfume!" Some celebrity scandals people remember for a long time.

It's hard to refer to emotional breakdowns as scandals, but when stars have them in public, they can take a serious toll on the public's perception of them. Amanda Bynes's 2013 Twitter meltdown, Britney Spears's self-coiffing in 2007, Sinéad O'Connor's Facebook episode, and Robert Downey Jr.'s tremendous fall in the 1990s all come to mind.[1] For Downey in particular, it didn't seem like he'd ever resume his career, but after he completed rehab, he stayed sober and did everything he could to return to work and clean living. Then he starred in *Iron Man* and went on to have one of the most successful second acts in movie history.

Some celebrity scandals have been more bizarre than life-threatening or dangerous, such as when Winona Ryder was caught in 2001 for shoplifting $5,560 in merchandise from the Beverly Hills Saks Fifth Avenue store. A security chief testified that she told him she'd been told to shoplift by a director in preparation for an upcoming role. This was actually not true. She later told *Interview* magazine that her arrest was a blessing in disguise, and that the embarrassing incident forced her to take a much-needed break from acting.

---

1. In May 2013, Bynes was arrested in New York for criminal possession of marijuana, attempted tampering with evidence, and reckless endangerment, and she underwent a psychiatric evaluation. Later that year, she was hospitalized for a mental-health evaluation hold and her parents filed for conservatorship of their daughter shortly after her hospitalization began. In 2007, Britney Spears shaved her head in a late-night incident in Tarzana, California, that was filmed. Sinéad O'Connor's unsettling Facebook posts in 2016 gave rise to worries that the Irish singer was suicidal. And Robert Downey Jr. had a succession of arrests (getting drunk in public, getting busted, ditching rehab, having his neighbors come home to find him blacked out in their son's bed).

That was not the case for the actress Sean Young, who had a promising career in the 1980s and then created a series of peculiar public disturbances, some of them while she was dressed in a homemade Catwoman suit.

The most common type of celebrity scandal, of course, is the sex scandal. They can be very bad and career-threatening or titillating and career-improving. The first celebrity sex scandal I recall in my lifetime had to do with Rob Lowe. In July 1988, Lowe was in Atlanta, Georgia, to attend the Democratic National Convention to support Michael Dukakis. While there, Lowe went to a nightclub with fellow Brat Packers Judd Nelson and Ally Sheedy, where he met two Atlanta hairdressers: one was twenty-two, the other sixteen, which was the legal age of consent in Georgia, although Lowe said later he had no idea she was that young. He brought them both back to his hotel room and [flashing bad-judgment alert] he filmed their activities on his video camcorder.

According to Lowe, he went to the bathroom, and when he came out, the girls were gone and had taken the tape with them. A few weeks later Lowe received a lawyer's letter informing him that the mother of the sixteen-year-old had the tape and was threatening to sue. Lowe's lawyers called it an extortion attempt, but he settled out of court with the girl and her father—not the estranged mother, who then went public with the tape.

I remember when this happened. It was bad. This was before celebrity sex tapes had their own section at Blockbuster (and when Blockbusters actually existed), and people's reactions to it boiled down to disgust. The whole situation looked as if the actor we loved in *The Outsiders, Class,* and *St. Elmo's Fire* had taken advantage of his celebrity with a couple of young local girls. Comments from film producers were that the tape would make it very hard for anyone to hire Lowe again. But they did. Years later, on *Oprah*, Lowe said he made one of the first celebrity sex tapes. And times had changed enough for him to joke, "Sometimes to be a trailblazer is highly overrated."

Lowe also denied knowing the girl was sixteen. He himself was twenty-two at the time, and the club checked his ID even though they knew who he was, so he said he never thought there would be underage girls there. He claims getting caught was the best thing that ever happened to him because it made him get sober. Clearly, this did not have a lasting negative effect on him, as he went on to enjoy a fabulous career including parts on the award-winning *West Wing* and *Parks and Recreation*.

When I talked to Jon Ronson, the author of *So You've Been Publicly Shamed*, about why he thought some people like Rob Lowe emerged from such scandals, he said, "If you're going to be in a sex scandal, make sure that it's consensual. Those you can recover from."

An equally high-profile sex scandal occurred in 1995 when Hugh Grant was arrested for lewd conduct with a prostitute named Divine Brown in Los Angeles. As a result, his LAPD mug shot became more recognizable than any of his publicity shots. It had a minor effect on his movie career, more humorous to people than anything, because of his gentlemanly, stuttering, very British persona and his willingness to appear on *The Tonight Show with Jay Leno* the next day. He made the obligatory apology: "Last night I did something completely insane . . . I have hurt people I love and embarrassed people I work with. For both things I am more sorry than I can ever possibly say." As a result, life and his career went on.

Eddie Murphy's similar situation in 1997 had an unfortunate twist. He was arrested with a prostitute in his car, but this one was a "known transsexual," according to the LA County Sherriff's Department. Eddie, of course, said he did not know this, that he only stopped to help a person with car trouble. He said, "I did nothing wrong. I was trying to be a good Samaritan and this is what happens."

For a while it was unclear whether Pee-wee Herman, the comedian and star of the hit children's TV show *Pee-wee's Playhouse*, would recover from his sex scandal. In case you missed it, Pee-wee Herman, whose real name is Paul Reubens, was visiting his parents in Sarasota, Florida, in July 1991. While there, he decided to catch a flick, the X-rated *Nurse Nancy* (which sounds to me like a *Pee-wee's Playhouse* character). In an unfortunate bit of timing, the police were operating a sting and they found Reubens allegedly playing with his private parts. It wasn't a huge deal—he was released on $219 bail—but then someone recognized him and the media took over. He was suddenly in the headlines, like "Kids' Show Star Arrested for Indecent Exposure."

CBS cancelled *Pee-wee's Playhouse*, Reubens agreed to pay a $50 fine plus $85 in court costs to Sarasota County, and he produced a thirty-second public service commercial for the Partnership for Drug-Free America. Although the records were sealed, the news was out and it appeared to be the end of Pee-wee's big adventures.

A couple of months later, Reubens appeared at the MTV Music Video Awards as Pee-wee. The audience was clearly in support of him, and warmly embraced him, but despite that, he decided not to play Pee-wee anymore and chose to use the opportunity to pursue other kinds of roles. Luckily for his fans (yours truly included), Pee-wee broke that promise, and in 2016 Netflix released a new film, *Pee-wee's Big Holiday*. Fans and critics alike embraced him in this return. In this case, he certainly didn't hurt anyone; it was that his image was so closely tied to his childlike charm.

That was not the case with actor Stephen Collins, who over the course of a bitter divorce was taped confessing to "inappropriate sexual conduct with minors," a revelation that effectively ended his career.

Or Eliot Spitzer, the married former New York attorney general and governor who hired prostitutes. Although he was male and the prostitutes were female and the arrangements were consensual, it was clearly illegal and Spitzer's former jobs were to uphold the laws of the state of New York and to prosecute the people who didn't. It was the ultimate betrayal of his constituents. We hate hypocrites.

Politicians are supposed to stand for something more. Or at least they were before the 2016 US presidential election, when the Electoral College chose the first reality-show host to be the nation's president—the forty-fifth—reigniting debates about illegal and unethical behavior in our nation's leaders and the disturbing rise of international meddling in US elections. It was the latest chapter in a string of instances of high-level political misconduct. Think of how scandal destroyed the presidential campaigns of Senators Gary Hart in the 1980s and John Edwards in 2008. One wonders if the actions of those men would

THE SORDID SPECTRUM OF CELEBRITY SCANDAL

have even moved the needle during the 2016 election, when it was revealed that Donald Trump was caught on tape bragging about grabbing women by the pussies. We were unforgiving of Anthony Weiner, the New York congressman who tweeted a picture of his own weiner and was found to be having phone sex (using the name Carlos Danger, which was a little extra gift to the tabloids) with a twenty-three-year-old woman. He got himself a prime spot in the Never Learns Hall of Fame when he did it again with someone even younger and got caught. And his name came up in the now-famous emails scrutinized by former FBI Director James Comey—emails that experts say cost Hillary Clinton the election. As the line between celebrity and government service gets blurrier, I sincerely hope such examples of terrible behavior are aberrations and not the new rule.

Then there is the category of celebrity scandal I call Train Wreck. I put a lot of people in this category. Some seem sadly troubled and appear to me to need professional help, probably medication, and definitely someone to take down their social media accounts, at least for a while. Others appear to be on some kind of controlled substance that affects their decision making. I sent Dr. Lisa Weinstock, a psychiatrist in Westchester County, New York, who has an interest in celebrity behavior, a video of Kanye West having a very strange rant on *The Ellen DeGeneres Show* that had gone viral to get her opinion of what's happening.

"It's hard to say whether his behavior in that clip represents a manic episode," Dr. Weinstock says, "because by definition a manic episode lasts one week and during that time the person has multiple symptoms, including grandiosity, decreased need for sleep, pressured speech, flight of ideas, distractibility, increased goal-directed activity, and impulsive, potentially dangerous behaviors. You don't have to have all of them, just three. But since we are only seeing a small period of time, we can't really say whether his behavior at the interview was part of a manic episode, since we don't know if he was just acting like that for the interview or if his behavior was part of a bigger, long-lasting period of time where he was acting in a similar fashion.

"Psychiatry is kind of annoying in the sense that since we don't have blood tests or X-rays to diagnose things; we do it with symptoms, and to be 'official'—and the 'official' definitions keep changing—bipolar 1 disorder is diagnosed when you have had a manic episode and no other explanation is available to explain it (e.g., drugs, medical problems, etc.). That said, he certainly was acting in ways that are not inconsistent with the way people act when they are manic. But some of his behavior didn't seem manic at all to me. So looking at that clip, at the beginning I was unimpressed and didn't think there was any evidence that he was behaving like someone in a manic episode. In fact he appeared more narcissistic to me. He seemed disconnected, almost apathetic, kind of not really making eye contact and almost distracted. Not very connected to Ellen. Then as the interview went on, his demeanor changed (around minute six, when he got into that whole rap thing). At that point he seemed more grandiose, egotistical, and inappropriate at times (all signs of someone who is manic). He didn't seem highly energized for most of the interview, though, which is what I often see in someone floridly manic—they usually talk really fast and change from subject to subject, but again that is the more extreme form.

Part of the time I felt like he was more like someone on drugs, other parts he seemed totally disinterested, and other times either narcissistic or maybe manic or hypomanic."

Dr. Weinstock admits that it's "hard to judge in a vacuum because we know about other inappropriate/grandiose/impulsive things he has done in the past (e.g., jumping on stage at the Video Music Awards when Taylor Swift won), but we also don't know if he was high then, or if it was narcissistic behavior or truly manic or hypomanic behavior."

I often wonder if someone needs a personality disorder in order to be a celebrity. I don't think a lot of regular people could handle the constant attention, the unrelenting hours, the huge and sometimes unexpected trials in the court of public opinion. I ask Dr. Weinstock if she sees a correlation between personality disorder and celebrity.

"I think it's really interesting and have thought about it a lot—the relationship between mental illness (particularly bipolar disorder) and celebrity," she says. "I do think a lot of celebrities (and in general, super-successful people) probably are on the 'bipolar spectrum.' In the past we saw bipolar disorder as more of one fixed problem, where people had periods of mania alternating with periods of depression. Now we recognize some people have bipolar 2 disorder, where they are never floridly manic but do have periods of hypomania. When someone is floridly manic, their symptoms are so severe they interfere with their functioning; they often get psychotic and usually end up hospitalized. When someone is hypomanic, which is kind of a milder version of mania, they can often be just super-productive, sleep less, have lots of interesting and creative thoughts. And so to me, it's no surprise that people with a tendency toward mania or hypomania may often be very successful in creative fields." She adds, "I am talking about celebrities who really deserve to be celebrities because of their artistic/creative talents . . . not celebrities like the Kardashians."

I wonder if celebrities are less likely to be diagnosed because the people around them are often "yessing" them when they are in these modes, or even benefiting from their being manic.

"I think so," Dr. Weinstock says. "A lot of artists are probably either officially bipolar or on the spectrum. I think the other issue you bring up confounds things a little bit because you are right, people tend to 'yes' celebrities and cater to their whims. Many celebrities, particularly actors, are also narcissistic, and those qualities can sometimes mirror manic symptoms—particularly the egomania, grandiosity, etc. There is a 'rule' in psychiatry that you can't really diagnose a personality disorder when someone is suffering from what we call an 'Axis 1' disorder—a manic episode, depressive episode, etc. But oftentimes in the real world people suffer from both."

Then there is the other aspect of people who run to watch these psychiatric events. One example of that is Sinéad O'Connor, who publicly announced on *Oprah* that she is bipolar and posted a series of long tirades on Facebook directed at her family members and threatening suicide. I watched as fans around the world offered support while internet trolls mocked her. I was heartbroken and a little embarrassed reading such personal postings by someone who clearly was not well. It felt a little like slowing down to look at a car accident. There's curiosity but there's also regret and self-loathing, too.

Dr. Weinstock posits that some people are unhappy in their own lives and envious of certain celebrities' lives, so there's a little schadenfreude—the enjoyment that comes when we see them fall. It's an ugly side of human nature. I think there's another interesting aspect to watching celebrities in crisis: People enjoy being indignant on a celebrity's behalf and defending them, because in some ways, it brings them into the celebrities' lives. Like a real friend.

I was thinking of such celebrity breakdowns in 2016 when I saw that Charlie Sheen was trending on Facebook. Though I haven't really had any interest in Charlie Sheen as an actor since *Platoon*, I found myself clicking on the link, which sent me to an article where I learned that Sheen's ex-wife Denise Richards was telling the world that he wasn't paying child support and had kicked her out of the house he'd bought for her and their children to live in. The article quoted texts that Sheen allegedly sent his daughter. "Have a merry Xmas with your loser f—s–t mom . . . your dad is a rock star genius . . . your mom is a p–s wart," one text reportedly read. In another he allegedly wrote, "I'm going to kill you and I'm going to kill your mom."

Before this outburst, it was well known that Sheen had struggled with significant drug and alcohol and control issues. No matter what the cause of these messages, it was really unfortunate to learn he'd sent them. This, to me, is the dark side of celebrity.

I wonder whether, in this era of global social media that offers instant communication, celebrities get into more trouble with direct access to the rest of us. Think of how many celebrities have posted unwisely on Facebook, Instagram, or Twitter, realized their mistakes, and then decided to delete their accounts. How does one try to get the virtual genie back into its bottle?

One of my favorite people in the world (with probably the best name in the world) is Bumble Ward, a top publicist in Hollywood. She's an English beauty with one of the best-looking French bulldogs I've ever come across. "I have all of the characteristics of a good publicist," Bumble says. "A type A personality and, unfortunately, being a people-pleaser, since there is a great deal of that demanded. I feel like if you had a fairly healthy upbringing, you won't want to go into publicity. If you've gotten enough love as a child, you don't have to search for it someplace else."

Publicity is a very different dynamic now than it used to be when, for example, a movie star's publicist could successfully hide a client's infidelity, sexuality, or addiction. Today there is a lot less control over information, and as a result there's a much greater need for crisis management.

One of Bumble's big clients is the writer and director Quentin Tarantino, who has a reputation for being a loose cannon. It is obviously difficult to work with someone who's unpredictable. What do you do when someone is both unpredictable and famous? You try to be prepared for every eventuality. How can anyone—a publicist, a manager, a journalist, a paparazzo—control the response to such a person's off-the-cuff ideas, or worse? The answer is, you can't.

"My job is to be the artist's advocate, to have the ability to really understand what they are trying to do and to let people know what that is, because they can't always articulate it themselves. The work and how they represent themselves with the work are two very different things, so my job is to see that that vision was really being seen."

Bumble has been called upon to do damage control for some of the biggest names around. I ask her whether she thinks of social media as a client nightmare. I know that publicists like to be in control of the stories their clients tell the media; I've interviewed many celebrities by phone over the years, only to realize the extra breathing I heard on the line belonged to a publicist waiting to bust in if the client stepped into a potential publicity minefield or I asked something that was off-limits.

"When you have a direct link to your audience, which is what Twitter, Instagram, and Facebook provide to a certain extent, I think you cut out any possibility of misinterpretation," Bumble says. "If you make a mistake, it's your mistake, but you do have this direct link with people. I think the good outweighs the bad. There are certainly people in the world who shouldn't be on social media, but it's not just confined to celebrities. There are some people who just aren't very good at it. If used properly, social media makes the message much clearer and more accessible and less prone to misinterpretation.

"I think it's quite lovely when you see people mucking up their own mess when they say after the fact, 'You know what, you misunderstood me. This is what I meant.' I think that direct link with the audience is a really cool thing."

While that is true, it's also true, as Bumble says, that some celebrities can't pull off that direct communication. Take celebrity chef Paula Deen. In 2012 Deen was sued by a former employee for racial discrimination and sexual harassment. She denied the accusations but admitted to using the N-word. Oh. OK. Shortly after that, Deen tweeted a picture of her son in brown-face pretending to be Desi Arnaz. I ask Bumble about the resulting uproar.

Bumble is very clear: "I feel really strongly about this. She [Deen] really screwed up. She came out with a video saying she's sorry, and you know she's only doing it because she knew the Food Network would dump her, and then they did. She only did something when she thought her business was crashing. No offense to the publicist handling that, but what were they thinking? The minute celebrities do something stupid, they need to own it. They need to stand up and don't pussyfoot around it. They need to take action. You have only a few moments where you basically show who you are. In these situations, you show you can take responsibility for your mistakes. When you get those moments and they're gone, they're gone."

As a result of Deen's actions and statements, at least twelve companies severed ties with her. A food empire lay in pieces.

"Another point about celebrities: they aren't out there in the real world. They are in a completely different world than the one you and I live in. They are so protected that they don't have access to a lot of the stuff we have access to and they are fed the information on an as-needed basis. And that's a real problem." Complications arise, Bumble notes, when these unthinking celebrities are let out of the bubble, unsupervised.

. . .

As with everything else celebrities do, when they screw up, the media coverage is extensive. People come out of the woodwork to tell the news media what they saw or heard. And what defines the "news media" has changed. It's no longer the *New York Times*, the *Los Angeles Times*, and *People*. It's the *Enquirer*, TMZ, and websites with axes to grind or clicks to get. Whenever I find a celebrity story on some site I've never heard of, the page is peppered with links to stories from other sites, like "Celebrities You Didn't Know Had a Conjoined Twin" or "Celebrities with the Most Disastrous Boob Jobs." The goal here is to get clicks, not to have journalistic integrity.

Then there are calls by the media and through social media to own up to this faux pas publicly. It's simply not what happens, say, when your neighbor got caught embezzling church funds. People everywhere suddenly know the details of what happened. Almost more important, they believe it's their right to know. This kind of unleashed, unfiltered information colors how we think about celebrities, and it affects celebrities' livelihoods, as well as the bit of life they hope to keep private. So it's key that they—and we—understand that it's crucial to think before speaking.

Celebrity gives people the opportunity to be heard. But they have to be careful that they are clear and the public is getting the right messages from them; there is no script.

We have very high expectations for celebrities and somehow hold them to a higher moral level, expecting them to be godlike though they are just mortals.

Intermission 11

For most of the '90s I worked as a foot messenger for a foreign-currency exchange in New York City

I remember once entering an upscale hat boutique on 61st Street and Madison Avenue (I believe it was Suzanne Newman's, since moved to Lexington and 61st) to collect a check, as Bill Cosby happened to be exiting. I was attempting to slip past him and into the store, but he thought I had stopped specifically to greet him. He paused in the doorway, blocking my entrance, and I suddenly found myself worried about Bill Cosby being embarrassed. What followed was a very awkward exchange where I had to kind of pander to his celebrity in order to do my shitty, low-paying job. It was a very odd five seconds in which I felt like I was paying a troll with my dignity to cross a bridge with a crappy view.

Bonus section: I worked at Barnes & Noble at the Grove in Los Angeles in 2005 (a great thing for one's self-esteem when you're in your late thirties and living in LA!), where I helped a wonderfully foulmouthed Melanie Griffith shop for yoga DVDs; had a possibly drunk Vince Vaughn loudly, but not unkindly, ask me where to find the book Rich Dad, Poor Dad; *rang up a snippy, white-glove-wearing Faye Dunaway; and had a brief moment making small talk with a supernice, down-to-earth George Carlin in the break room while he was waiting to begin a book signing.*

—TED TRAVELSTEAD

★

In my former life I was a professional wrestler, traveling three hundred days a year, averaging four flights per week. No wonder some strange shit has happened to me on planes. Southwest Airlines is usually the worst offender. This airline is a microcosm of infantile behavior. Patrons save seats with sweaters, avoid eye contact, and require an annual cooties shot, so I always anticipate the worst when I'm forced to fly it. On a 5 a.m. flight home to Tampa, Florida, I groggily dragged my carry-on roller bag, a Starbucks coffee taller than my torso, and a shoulder-length messenger bag to the only available seats at the back of the plane. I waddled down the aisle of the plane like a delirious bag lady. As I reached an empty row, I began to question how I was going to successfully lift my carry-on into the overhead bin while one of my hands was filled with scalding-hot life juice. Now, I consider myself a strong woman, but this was a pickle. While a queue of people also trying to make their way to the empty seats impatiently waited behind me, I tripped over my own feet trying to place my jumbo coffee on my desired seat's armrest. My messenger bag had swung toward my stomach, pulling me forward like an anchor. While I tried to regain my footing, a man shuffled uncomfortably close to my back. "Excuse me," I said, without looking at the creep, "I still have to throw this bag up there and I need a little room."

"Uhnnnnnnnnnffff," Creep responded.

I whipped the messenger bag behind me to help steady my stance and also so there was at least some sort of barrier between the groaning man and my ass crack. "I don't want to accidentally hit you with my suitcase, guy."

"Fuuuuurrrmanbluuuurgggg," somehow managed to escape the hungry zombie's mouth. With the motion of a power lifter's clean and jerk, I lifted the bag above my head and into the bin, wedging my hand between the roller bag and the floor of the overhead bin. As I tried to wriggle it free, I could hear the man exasperatedly sigh and try to advance forward anyway. He apparently assumed he possessed the ability to pass through my body, which, frankly, would've been less disturbing than the unintelligible sounds he continued to make.

"Can you give me a second, dude?" I began to shout as I yanked my hand free. In what seemed like slow motion, my fist flew backward and directly against the strange man's mouth. I turned around aghast and worried I had just knocked his teeth out. The impact was so forceful his entire body tipped to the side and back into place like a drunk-ass Weeble wobbling. "Oh my God, are you OK?!" I said as I met the glazed-over eyes of Ron Jeremy.

As the flight went on, I began to swell with pride, as I had inadvertently done the female race a solid. Then I realized my hand had touched Ron Jeremy's mouth. I went into the tiny bathroom and cut my hand off at the wrist. I have a hook now.

—AJ MENDEZ BROOKS

TWELVE

ON LOCATION

★

I used to have lunch with a friend of mine every few months at a little restaurant in Manhattan's West Village called Sant Ambroeus. The West Village is, by nature, charming. The landmark buildings up and down the tree-lined streets are small and well cared for, there are window boxes filled with bright red geraniums during the warm seasons, and life there is generally quiet. I'm always a little early for lunch and my friend is always a little late, so I would usually wait outside the restaurant for her. The restaurant is on the corner of Perry Street and there was always a noticeably loud gaggle of tourists, usually foreign, taking pictures in front of one of the street's lovely brownstones, which, while pretty, isn't appreciably different from the other buildings on the block. My friend and I would always spend a minute speculating on what the attraction was before going in for lunch.

Once when I was leaving, I noticed that there was a chain across the bottom of the brownstone's front steps. I decided to investigate the next time I was there. I ended up standing by a crowd of Japanese tourists where I heard, mixed in with the Japanese, the English words *"Sex and the City."* Then it hit me: This was the exterior to the brownstone that Carrie Bradshaw lives in. Or rather the exterior that was used as the Upper East Side building that was supposed to house her apartment, which was actually located in Silvercup Studios in Long Island City. I was amazed that this was a stop on a tour bus, because honestly, who cares? Also, while these tourists were looking at the inanimate building, they actually missed Academy Award–winner Sally Field and rock legend Mick Jagger (not together) walking by.

I completely understand the value of visiting the Gettysburg Battlefield or the Lorraine Motel in Memphis or the Colosseum in Rome. But the exterior of a building that Sarah Jessica Parker as Carrie Bradshaw "lives in"? That I don't understand. Which prompted me to think about places in New York City where I've seen people posing for pictures. What is it about physical places that we come to think of as connected to celebrity?

In my own neighborhood of New York's Upper West Side near Columbia University, there is a significant TV landmark, Tom's Diner, which is not only the subject of a Suzanne Vega song but also the outside of Monk's from the hit TV show that will never, ever leave syndication, *Seinfeld*. A lot of visitors to New York go there, too, and not just on the Kramer bus tour. (Kenny Kramer, the inspiration for Cosmo Kramer, conducts Kramer's Reality Tour, on which you can visit many of the sites from the TV show.) Tom's was my daughter's favorite restaurant before she knew its provenance. It then fascinated her that people stood outside Tom's and took selfies in front of it and didn't even go in for the delicious hamburger deluxe or its famous New York mystery shake.

Café Lalo on West 83rd was where a big scene from Nora Ephron's *You've Got Mail* was filmed. A scene in *Sea of Love* with Ellen Barkin and Al Pacino was filmed in a Korean deli that was around the corner from my apartment on 80th Street and Amsterdam Avenue, and I always felt like I should be wearing a trench coat with nothing underneath and stilettos when I shopped there, instead of my usual pajama pants and giant puffy coat. The Apthorp is where Meryl Streep's character lives in *Heartburn*, and the Dakota where Mia Farrow, John Cassavetes, Ruth Gordon, and Satan's spawn live in *Rosemary's Baby*. The 21 Club and Central Park's Sheep Meadow are both places Michael Douglas's character acts like a douche with a cell phone the size of a payphone in *Wall Street*. Of course downtown there is Katz's Delicatessen, the spot where Meg Ryan notoriously fakes an orgasm in *When Harry Met Sally*; the now-closed FAO Schwarz, home of the big piano on which Tom Hanks and Robert Loggia play "Chopsticks" in *Big*; the Russian Tea Room, where Dustin Hoffman as Dorothy Michaels and her agent, George Fields (played by the movie's director, Sydney Pollack) lunch; and of course 55 Central Park West, which is where all hell breaks loose in *Ghostbusters*. (Though to be clear, everyone thinks every old apartment building in New York City looks like that building—especially if you throw in some ominous clouds.)

New York isn't the only place with fabulous movie locations. Travel to Iowa and you can stand on the field from *Field of Dreams*. (I'm actually dying to see it, and as my boyfriend is from Iowa I don't know what's taking me so long.) In Los Angeles, the Biltmore Hotel is where *Chinatown*, *Beverly Hills Cop*, *Bachelor Party*, *True Lies*, *Dave*, *Ocean's Eleven*, *The Nutty Professor*, and *Fight Club* all filmed scenes. The Stanley Hotel in Estes Park, Colorado, is where *The Shining* was filmed (and where guests regularly claim to see ghosts). I also get chills on the Long Island Expressway whenever I pass the exit to Amityville, New York (of *Amityville Horror* fame). (For God's sake, Get Out!)

I decided to ask people taking a picture of themselves in front of Tom's Restaurant why they were doing it. One morning I stationed myself in front of Tom's, at the corner of Broadway and 112th Street. I didn't have to wait long. About thirty Scottish footballers—soccer players to Americans—showed up to take turns posing in front of the iconic eatery. I asked them why they were doing this. It turned out one of them had been passing by after an event at Columbia University, a few blocks north, and snapped a picture and posted it on Facebook. He got so many likes from his followers that his teammates all wanted their own shots. The original poster showed me: 325 likes and a list of comments along the line of "Say hi to Jerry for me" (though when he read it to me, he pronounced it "Jitty"). The coach said his players had been keeping an eye out for celebrities since they came to New York and hadn't seen any, but this diner was like a celebrity to them.

I finally realized what was driving the desire. When you're photographed in a famously filmed location, you can get a brief feeling of being the celebrity. When I sit at Tom's/Monk's, I can think about Elaine's Big Salad. If I swung my Manolos over my shoulder, I could walk up Carrie's steps and hear myself typing out my profound lesson of the day. Or when I'm at the top of the Empire State Building, a romantic location even if it had no film connections, I can be Meg Ryan waiting for Tom Hanks in *Sleepless in Seattle*. We are connected, the famous and the mundane, if just for a moment.

Intermission 12

When I was in high school I went to LA with my mom and dad. We stayed at the Beverly Hilton hotel.

The first day we were there, my mother and I went to the pool. While I was frying in the sun, my mother came over to me and said, "Which one is Lloyd Bridges?" I looked around at the pool and, sure enough, Lloyd Bridges was swimming in the pool. It was just before his big TV show, Sea Hunt, where he did a lot of underwater swimming.

I pointed him out and my mother jumped into the pool and swam over to him. "I've been in LA for two weeks and you're the first star I've seen," she said. He said, "Too bad it had to be someone like me." She said, "Oh, I'm excited anyway!" Then she proceeded to spend the rest of the afternoon on a chaise with the Bridges family. I stayed away.

—MARCIA KLAM

★

I was about to board the downtown 2 train at 96th Street after therapy one afternoon when I saw a scruffy guy whom I immediately recognized as Philip Seymour Hoffman. I debated for a few minutes about whether to approach him, but we both smiled at each other, so I thought, what the hell, and just started talking to him. He was working on True West *at the time, on Broadway. I remember telling him—and this was true—that I'd just been talking about him to someone he knew, and I felt like I wasn't so surprised to look up and see him there. I was thirty, had a level of chutzpah I've since lost. Anyway, it didn't matter, we just naturally fell into a conversation really easily as we waited for the train and eventually boarded. He asked what I did for a living and I told him I was a book critic at the time. He told me he had just wrapped a film in which he portrayed Lester Bangs, and soon we were talking about the lost art of criticism and what made Bangs great even when he took someone apart like Patti Smith (i.e., Easter—he knew she was capable of masterpieces and this wasn't it) and someone like* New York *magazine's then theater critic John Simon (who panned him so cruelly in* True West*) so bad. And then we got to 42nd Street–Times Square, and we had to part ways. He got up and said he'd see me around soon in that way that people do when they actually expect to, and I kind of thought we would run into each other again. We never did. But it was one of my favorite encounters with any stranger, famous or mortal, ever.*

—KERA BOLONIK

THIRTEEN

THE SHELF LIFE OF A CELEBRITY ATHLETE

★

For all the billions of people whose life goal is to be famous, there are a few who have gotten there accidentally. Erica Jong was a literary novelist and poet who in 1973 published an iconic, bestselling, paradigm-changing novel, *Fear of Flying*.

"I wrote the book, I'm living with my family, and then all of a sudden, I've got people camped out in front of my apartment building wanting to meet me and be me," she said. "I was catatonic! It isn't something they prepare you for in graduate school!"

Four decades after the publication of *Fear of Flying*, Erica Jong is still a famous author. Today there are very few writers who are household names, but back in the 1970s, some writers were treated differently. Jong was on every talk show, newspaper and magazine articles were written about her, and she was invited to movie premieres and was treated like royalty.

"It's a weird thing, because [celebrity] has nothing to do with the work. It has everything to do with *your* work, but it's not the life of a writer, which is solitary and serious and internal. Fame means millions of people have the wrong idea of who you are. And there's nothing you can do about it."

But that was then; this is now. Writers today generally don't find themselves on the cover of *People*. If you're in high school and are an exceptionally talented young writer, you might be favored by your teachers and maybe win a prize, but generally you are not going to be voted prom queen because of your artistic gifts.

That is not the case for great young athletes. I remember how star athletes in my junior high and high school *were* our versions of celebrities. I would look at my brother's friends the way I looked at young heartthrobs in magazines: They were talented, handsome, unattainable—and the ones who went on to play sports in college were even more celebrated. I remember reading about the huge number of fan letters Herschel Walker received when he played football at the University of Georgia. He was arguably the most popular college sportsman of his time.

Looking back on those days, I wonder if celebrity athletes who've been treated as special at such a young age are better prepared for celebrity than actors. It's not the same as being a child star, as a young athlete gets attention gradually and it's not quite "movie set" levels of attention.

Unlike actors or politicians, athletes are like superheroes: they can physically do things that the rest of us can't. In theory we could learn lines to appear in a play or get ourselves elected mayor, but very few of us can run one hundred meters in less than ten seconds or dunk a basketball or do a backflip on a balance beam. Athletes' amazing physical skills make them famous, and we admire them for ability we can never hope to emulate. Which is why it's such a thrill for many of us when we meet a sports hero in person.

Take Michael Strahan, a retired defensive end for the New York Giants and the former cohost of *Live with Kelly and Michael* as an example. Watch how even jaded stars react to being interviewed by him. It certainly isn't the way they reacted to Regis Philbin, who originated the show with Kathie Lee Gifford back in the 1980s. Strahan was on the red carpet for the Academy Awards a few years ago, and he stopped Dustin Hoffman for an interview. Dustin Hoffman is not known as a man who loves the press. And yet when he talked to Strahan, he looked like a little kid meeting Santa. During the interview Hoffman even mentioned a play that Strahan had made while a Giant, and the Oscar winner giddily answered all of Strahan's dopey red-carpet questions. Right there at the Oscars, the magic of the star athlete was laid bare for all to see.

My brother Matthew, in addition to being a terrific novelist and short-story writer, has written a fair amount of journalism. In 2007, he wrote a piece for GQ on Rafael Nadal, then the number two tennis player in the world. A year later he interviewed Robert Downey Jr. He said walking with them out in the world were completely different experiences. In Miami, women ran through traffic to get to Rafa: They'd grab him and kiss him. They adored him! In Los Angeles, Robert Downey Jr. and my brother had no problem going through crowds or eating sushi; people noticed Downey but left him alone. He believed it was that Rafa was larger than life—people could not resist him. Downey was resistible, and maybe his LA fans were a little accustomed to seeing a famous actor walking among them.

In those days my brother and I spoke on the phone a lot, and we had a long conversation when he was in Miami with Rafa. I remember his saying that professional athletes were like superpeople. Everything on them is bigger, their bodies and heads. And tennis players, he said, "have these hands, yellowed with thick calluses you could drive a nail through" and "the deepest tan, like they spend their life in this war under the sun." When I asked him what Rafa's personality was like, he said, "I don't know—he's like a kid." (At the time, Nadal was actually twenty, which, from where I sit, *is* a kid.) Matt said Rafa was reading a young adult novel and he was having a really hard time with English. He was a horrible driver (he almost ran people over) but insisted on taking the wheel. He drove them to the tennis center in Key Biscayne, and they pulled into a space right next to Novak Djokovic, who rolled down his window and let out a primitive funny scream that Nadal answered. They were two friends, happy to see each other.

In the house we grew up in, we had a tennis court and we also had a cottage we rented out. For many years, the renter was a tennis pro with a local racket club. He personally trained a couple of young star tennis players. I would hear them practicing on our court every weekday at 5 a.m. for two hours before school. Nadal was a young star and came from a family of professional athletes, so he undoubtedly had similar training. This is not the case with a kid who is just pretty good at football or baseball or soccer and plays in school and practices with his team. The young world-class tennis player has a coach, intense practices, and his own tournament schedule. The kids in training that I knew were never at school dances or Saturday football games, and the adults around them were needing this "thing" from them: they needed them to be focused and to win, and there was a lot invested in them. So they just weren't able to give them much free time. It stands to reason that they don't develop in every way at the rate of a kid who spends his free time (mostly) the way he wants.

I was talking about celebrity athletes with Esther Newberg, my agent. She represents successful athletes and sportswriters and is a huge college basketball and professional baseball fan. I was complaining about how obnoxious professional athletes can become when they get famous, giving former baseball player José Canseco as an example. Or Johnny Manziel, the Heisman Trophy–winning former quarterback who has struggled publicly with addiction issues and was accused by his ex-girlfriend of abuse.

Esther thought I needed to speak to a smart, thoughtful professional athlete about the idea of celebrity in sport. "You need to meet R. A. Dickey," she said.

I am a fan of baseball. A very big fan. Especially old baseball and baseball as mythology. Some of my favorite movies are *Field of Dreams, Bull Durham, The Natural,* and *Eight Men Out.* My walls are filled with baseball art, and I have two large bookshelves filled with great baseball books, fiction and nonfiction, picture and coffee-table books. My favorite museum exhibit of all time was called "Diamonds Are Forever: Artists and Writers on Baseball." I even wrote a screenplay about what would happen if the 1927 Yankees came back and saved baseball.

R. A. Dickey played for the Mets from 2010 to 2012, and New York loved him. He was like the old-time ballplayers, a real, true-blue good guy, with excellent facial hair and a terrific story of reinventing himself after an injury and becoming one of the best knuckleball pitchers of all time, winning the Cy Young Award. Over three seasons and sixty-three starts in New York, Dickey had a 3.18 ERA (earned run average) and a solid 1.212 WHIP (walks plus hits per innings pitched). He showed a unique ability to change speeds with his knuckleball, ranging from the low 60s all the way up to the mid-80s. In short, he was amazing.

My brother Brian, a Mets fan among Mets fans, was heartbroken when Dickey was traded from New York to the Toronto Blue Jays. So he was excited to learn I'd have a chance to sit down with Dickey, who'd agreed to meet me. When I was setting up the interview, R.A. and I texted each other, so I forwarded this back-and-forth with R.A. to Brian. Suddenly he was twelve again.

(R.A. said he'd be happy to talk to me on one of his trips to New York. I asked him which trip would work best for him, and he said, "I'll leave it up to you to get in touch with me. It gets real busy for me real soon." I forwarded the email to Brian with the note, "We know why it gets real busy." And Brian wrote back, "Because pitching baseballs." There's almost nothing that is as fun as texting with Brian when the Mets are winning.)

The day before I was scheduled to interview R.A., I texted him to ask about where and when to meet. When I didn't hear from him, I assumed the meeting was off. That was fine, because it was the day my daughter was graduating from fifth grade and there was a big commencement ceremony at school and a lunch and my mother was coming with me, so I was kind of a basket case. Not since my daughter had graduated from preschool and kindergarten had I been this moved.

So that morning at school, as I sat between my ex-husband and my mother watching dozens of fifth graders get their diplomas and dropping tears on my new linen dress that turned out to be see-through when it gets wet, I got a text from R.A. apologizing and asking if I could meet him at his hotel at 2 p.m. that afternoon. I had a little panic attack because I was there at my daughter's graduation, sobbing like Kate Winslet having just let go of Leo in *Titanic*, and now I suddenly had to change gears and leave early.

I had mixed feelings about leaving my daughter's end-of-elementary-school commencement before it was over, but I also knew that it was gracious of R.A. to make time in his schedule to speak with me before heading to Citi Field to play the Mets. I told myself it was a good example to show my daughter that sometimes her mother had to work. So off I went.

I got to R.A.'s hotel and I saw other players in the lobby and it was kind of crazy. When I worked at *Late Night with David Letterman*, Dave once took me to a Knicks game and we sat courtside, where I was spellbound by the size of the men. Baseball players look slightly more normal, but there was still a sort of radiance about them. I think it's the glow of celebrity mixed with amazing physical prowess, with a little Aramis thrown in for good measure.

I went to R.A.'s room and he let me in. He was alone, and his iPhone was playing big-band music. He apologized that he was in the middle of getting dressed and packing and said if it was OK, he would try to do two things at once. We laughed, because he is the antithesis of the clichéd dumb jock.

My first question was, "In no other line of work is your physical self sort of the product the way it is in professional sports. No other person being interviewed would be asked 'How is your groin?' and expect an answer. So what does it feel like to have your body somewhat up for grabs?"

He nodded and said, "That is a very insightful question, wow." (I tell you this because instead of writing down his answer, I wrote down, "That is a very insightful question, wow." I mention this for two reasons: One, I don't need to write down quotes about me in an interview [duh], and two, I never take notes during an in-person interview, because I tape all my interviews. But I needed something to do with my hands because I was so nervous: This was R. A. Dickey I was talking to. Celebrity can affect even us hard-boiled journalists.)

"The mainstream media just doesn't get that I have nothing to hide behind. It's just me. I am pretty transparent in interviews, but I have boundaries. And someone knows by the look I give to a question if I'm not going there."

I ask him about the perks of being a celebrity. "The benefits are that I have a platform to say certain things. There are a lot of smart people that have stuff to say, but people listen to me, and that's a pretty cool thing."

He supports a number of charities, which he gives a tremendous amount of time to, and he doesn't just slap his name on them. After the 2011 season, against the wishes of the New York Mets organization, Dickey climbed Mount Kilimanjaro in Tanzania. The inherent risks of mountain climbing, combined with the wording of Dickey's baseball contract, meant that if he got injured during the climb, he would have been cut from the team and would lose his $4.25 million 2012 salary. Undaunted by this possibility, Dickey climbed 19,341 feet to reach Uhuru Peak, the highest point in Africa. His efforts raised more than $130,000 and awareness for the Bombay Teen Challenge, an organization that rescues and cares for human-trafficking victims in India.

While having a soapbox to draw attention to important causes is laudable, I want to know about the real perks of being a sports celebrity—the champagne baths, the free sports cars. He chuckles. "I'm on the road a lot. Away from my wife and kids. We play one hundred and sixty-two games a year, so the best thing in the world to me is being home with my wife and kids. And when I'm home, I just like taking out the garbage and being a normal person. On the road, sure, I've got a guy coming up here to put my bag on the bus—I don't have to do that. It's a weird thing because [baseball] is such a dysfunctional life. You don't really have close friends except other athletes. There's just not a lot of time or opportunity [to do anything else], or people who really understand what your life is like, what you're going through. We are our own ecosystem. But baseball is a very relational game. You have relationships with the coaches, the batboys, and you're very close to the players."

What about baseball fans? People don't scream profanities at singers for missing notes or actors for doing a bad Irish brogue.

But go to just about any game—baseball, football, basketball, hockey—and listen to the shouts of "ya bum" and worse. It's unique and I wonder if it bothers players.

R.A. nods. "Sure, there are things that piss you off—I'm human. But I empathize with fans. Their teams are very important to them. They take your failing very personally. I know—I'm a fan, too!"

The great appeal of attending a baseball game, R.A. says, is that it's "a singular experience. You can go to a game, watch an inning, have a conversation, get a beer. The game isn't going to pass you by. It's right there with you.

"Another thing, you can get closer to the players then you can with other sports," he adds. "If your kid has a favorite ballplayer, you can go see them at spring training, get a ball signed."

Listening to R.A. talk about baseball, I can hear in my head the soundtrack from *Field of Dreams*. I remember the scene when Kevin Costner says to himself in disbelief, "I'm pitching to Shoeless Joe Jackson!" I know just how he feels. Here I am interviewing a great ballplayer about celebrity, and what I really want to know is if he feels the way I do about baseball.

So I do what the prize-winning investigative journalists do: I ask.

"Oh yeah." He smiles slightly. "The smell of the grass, the sounds, the lights—I get the mythology. It really bums me out when I see ballplayers acting like dumb jocks, chasing tail. You know, my kids are baseball fans. I don't want them to see that."

It turns out R.A. loves the novel *The Natural* by Bernard Malamud, too. "Such rich writing," he says. His phone rings and he answers it, telling the person he can come and get his stuff. I stand up and take the only selfies I've ever taken on any interview I've ever done in my whole life. We look at them and they're blurry. I ask R.A. to do them again and he does. Because he's the baseball version of a mensch.

When I leave the hotel, I immediately call my brother Brian. I sit on a bench and get the recorder ready to play him a little of R.A. talking. I hit the Play button and there's nothing there. I have recorded nothing.

After using some of the profanity R.A. doesn't want his kids to hear at a baseball game, I sit down and fill in everything I left out of my notes. For a second I marvel at the fact that I took notes at all. And then I tell myself that if this were 1908 and I was interviewing Walter "the Train" Johnson—trust me, a very famous baseball player back then—I would not have had an iPhone recording it. Still. It's the 21st century, and I am ready to slit my wrists.

I'm sure that the nerves from my daughter's graduation and the corresponding guilt of leaving early and the excitement of sitting down with a real ballplayer are to blame for the flub. As I walk away, I am sure I hear someone shout, "Ya bum!"

I head home and on the way I realize the irony of how quickly I lost R. A. Dickey's interview, because that's how I see celebrity athletes. One twist of an ankle, one hit from behind, one fall, can derail a career in a split second. As much as anyone can try to take care of themselves—smart training, icing the knee, eating well, not drinking—we cannot control our bodies or the bodies of those around us. It makes it almost understandable why some of them succumb to drugs to prolong their careers. With athletes the stakes are so much higher, and we watch them more closely and more intensely than we do any other kind of celebrity. At any moment, their celebrity lives can end. Like the dragonflies of the celebrity world, they are breathtakingly beautiful and gone too soon.

Intermission 13

I'm not usually wowed by celebrities but one morning when I was working at an outdoor farmers' market, I spotted a disheveled man in his early seventies beelining across the grounds. He was stumbling ahead almost on tiptoe, as if pulled forward by the weight of his own monumental head. That head was immediately recognizable, equal parts Ben Franklin, Albert Einstein, and Frankenstein's monster— cavernous eye sockets, twin thickets of eyebrows, an intensely topographical brow, all crowned by tufts of frazzled white hair striking out in every direction.

"William Kunstler!" I shouted. He froze and turned, eyeing me with a look of wary resignation. Then he started toward me.

I grew up in a small New York town not far from Green Haven prison, home to "Old Sparky," the state's last remaining electric chair. Its dreadful proximity came in handy whenever one of my older brothers wanted to fill me with terror and bend me to his will. "Do it now or Mom's gonna take you to Green Haven!" It wasn't till my teen years that the lingering chill dissipated, when a high-profile ACLU lawyer rode into town to challenge and ultimately defeat the state's bid to put a serial offender to death. It was Kunstler. His face was all over the national news and his name was cursed all over the local streets. He was a meddler and an agitator, a "Commie kike" and a "Negro-loving liberal." He was a hero.

I watched him approach, his skeptical eyes patiently gathering me in. Then it occurred to me what he must be seeing: another angry farmer's son about to rip into him for a lifetime of "un-American" activity. I immediately stuck out my hand. He grabbed it, still dubious. "Thank you, Mr. Kunstler," I stammered. He was perplexed. "Thank you . . . for . . . defending . . . our liberties."

His expression smoothed into an ear-splitting grin, a joyous, disbelieving bark escaped him, and before I knew it, I was engulfed in a bear hug and yanked clean off my feet. The great William Kunstler was swinging me side to side a foot in the air and quaking with laughter. Eventually he put me down, grabbed both my shoulders, and fixed his watery eyes squarely on mine. "Thank you," he rasped, "thank you." Then he turned and hurried off.

—PAUL LEO

★

A million years ago, I was engaged (later married) to a movie producer, and we attended the royal premiere of Apollo 13 *in London. Before the movie was shown, we stood in a receiving line at a West End theater to greet Diana, the princess of Wales, who wore a hot little black dress, her ensemble in the spirit of more earthbound recent divorcées, which she was*

*in the process of becoming (she and Prince Charles were di-
vorced the next year).*

*Princess Diana was tall, lithe, lovely, and warm, even
more luminous in person than in photographs. We watched
the movie and afterward headed in limousines to a nearby
restaurant, where Hollywood royalty would mix with the real
thing.*

*Before the meal, we packed into an anteroom next to the
dining room, and I happened to circulate close to the princess's orbit as she hovered near a table filled with appetizers
(I can often be found next to food). Even though I was catatonic with nervousness, a common deer caught in royal head-
lights, to not say something would have been even more
awkward. I poked around at conversation (she was surpris-
ingly easy to talk to, as many have attested) but was inter-
rupted (saved?) when a movie star's wife bubbled on about
vacation homes and the princess was engulfed in a glittering,
animated circle. I shrank back and focused on finger food. I
didn't know from vacation homes, but I know my appetizers.*

*When we were released into the dining room, I hunted
for my name card among the long, rectangular tables, rows
of beautifully set china and polished silver, starched white
napkins. Ah. Found it. Good. My fiancé was seated next to
me. I could relax.*

*Then I noticed the card across the narrow table. Princess
Diana was to be seated directly in front of the girl who knew
nothing about vacation homes or, say, yachts. Seated next to
her was the movie star, his wife on the other side, where the
topic of vacation homes could not be so easily broached.*

I was on a date with Princess Diana.

She walked in. The collective side eye directed at yours truly practically burned as she took her place across from me. I didn't choose the seat, *I wanted to say to everybody.* The seat chose me.

I went for it.

I asked her about her boys. The older one, William, had just been sent to boarding school. Her eyes lit up when she talked about her children. Then I moved on to other pertinent questions, such as why were there no frozen yogurt shops in London. She agreed that we must do something about this grievous oversight. We jumped from topic to topic, the movie star, my fiancé, and I, just having a cozy chat with a princess. Later, I boldly tried to fix her up with a wealthy businessman I knew in Idaho. I yentaed the princess of Wales. (She was politely noncommittal.)

Right after the princess offered to share her dessert with my fiancé, as she was the first served, she told us she had to leave and warned us that the moment would seem strange. She rose.

We all stood. The room went silent. We held our collective breath and watched as she stepped outside, slightly hunched, as though hiding from the attention as the juggernaut of photographers lurched at her.

She was a breath of fresh air, more "normal" than anyone else in that room. It was like having dinner with a friend you've known for years, like an old girlfriend, or a sister. And I don't think she ever mentioned a vacation home.

—GIGI LEVANGIE GRAZER

FOURTEEN

REMEMBER MY NAME

★

Death happens to everyone, even celebrities. But when a celebrity dies, it's different. There is what feels like a global sadness, a universal mourning, and instead of one small community being affected, thousands of people collectively grieve.

When my boyfriend and I were planning a trip to Paris, I was pretty loose about what I wanted to do. I knew I didn't want to visit a lot of museums. I liked seeing iconic places, like the Eiffel Tower and the Seine and Pont des Arts. Just being on those charming city streets and strolling past shops and sitting at cafés would make me feel like I'm in *An American in Paris*. (I broke my museum rule once to go to the Louvre, because it's always been my dream to be forty feet from the *Mona Lisa* behind a sea of hundreds of tourists holding up selfie sticks and ignoring the No Photography sign.)

The one place I definitely wanted to visit was Père-Lechaise Cemetery, where many of the great and the famous are buried. My friend Kera, a fan of graveyards, calls it "a block party for the dead," which is my kind of party.

I don't know what I expected, maybe a marquee with the names of the dead in lights, but when I got there, Père-Lechaise looked just like every other old cemetery. At the entrance was a man selling maps to the graves of the famous, who reminded me of a guy on Sunset Boulevard in Los Angeles who sells maps to the stars' homes. These homes, though, were the forever kind. We didn't buy the map because we figured there were so many tour groups wandering around in there we could figure out where the A-listers were located. When I say "A-listers," I'm talking about Oscar Wilde, Jim Morrison, Gertrude Stein, Alice B. Toklas, and Isadora Duncan, not to mention Honoré de Balzac, Maria Callas, Collette, Chopin, Edith Piaf, Proust, and Richard Wright. These people were celebrities for acting, writing, singing, performing, dancing, composing—they created things that made them famous.

As we walked through, we both felt a reverence. We noted such a vast number of graves in disrepair: they were cracked and overgrown with vines. They looked like no one had attended them in a hundred years. Many of the inscriptions were hard to read, and the once-exquisite elaborate statues and mausoleums were in poor condition. I wondered how long it had been since someone had visited them—visited them on purpose, I mean, not like me, who was just stopping by on the way to see the Lizard King.

The first important grave we came to was Oscar Wilde's. When we arrived, there was a large tour group in front of it laughing heartily. Wilde's tomb is enormous, with a statue of a flying nude angel; its walls were covered in red lipstick kisses until his descendants erected a seven-foot glass wall to keep the stone from eroding from the cosmetic damage, to the deep disappointment of admirers. Still, it's an impressive site and seems worthy of the eminently quotable Wilde, writer and celebrity because of his art and his life. It's also the complete antithesis of neighbor Gertrude Stein's grave. Marked by a simple stone with her name and a small bed of rocks that visitors have formed into the shape of hearts, it seemed an absolutely fitting final resting place.

We walked to find Édith Piaf's grave, which is near those of the rest of her family. On the way we stopped to lay stones on the monuments to people killed in the Nazi death camps during World War II. We walked in silence until we hit the curious little circus that is Jim Morrison's grave. I'm neither a Doors fan nor a Jim Morrison fan, but I remember my brother reading *No One Here Gets Out Alive* when we were in high school and seeing in it pictures of Morrison's headstone in Paris. It seemed very cool and distant to me then. Now, standing in front of it, it looked small and sad. There was a fence around it so no one could picnic there, which had been a popular activity in years past. Some young girls were arguing with the only guard we saw in the place, because they had a bottle of wine with them. I wondered who paid for the security.

For as long as my friend Jancee and I have known each other, we have always connected when a celebrity dies. When we were younger and single and childless, we talked several times a day. It's harder now to talk even once a week, but a celebrity death always mandates a phone call.

I tend to learn before she does when someone famous has passed away because I'm addicted to social media. Depending on who it is, I might email her; the subject line is the celebrity's name and the email says, "We hardly knew ye." If it's someone bigger, more important to us both, it's a call. I knew she was at her parents' house in New Jersey in 2012 when Whitney Houston died, so I called her on her cell phone, which was a big deal for her. We both still have home answering machines, so a call to her cell means This Is Big. And it was. Whitney. One of the greatest singers on the planet. We'd both watched Whitney grow from *Seventeen* magazine model to top recording artist. When we were younger we could act out every step of her videos. We were at the Grammys together when she performed. To us, Whitney was the '80s and she was our age. We felt truly devastated.

During the call Jancee said, "Now it's going to start happening."

I knew what she meant. You hit an age when your death would be tragic, but not as tragic as it would've been if you'd died ten years before.

Jancee was working at *Rolling Stone* when Kurt Cobain died in 1994, and she knew everything before I did, and I heard details when they were only rumors. She updated me throughout the day.

When I think back to the shock of the death of Michael Jackson in 2009, I can hear her voice on the other end of the line singing "Ben." I remember when we talked about the fact that Farrah Fawcett, who died the same day Michael did, was going to get a little shafted in terms of attention. The same thing happened to Jim Henson, who died on the same day as Sammy Davis Jr. Who gets top billing on joint deaths depends on who sells the most magazines and which one the media thinks more people are interested in hearing about.

My brother Brian has some interesting insights about how we confront our feelings when famous people die.

"When a celebrity is dead, it's the only time we are better than they are," he said. Which is true—to a point. Except that Michael Jackson made $160 million in 2015 and Madonna made only $120 million. So maybe not from every perspective.

Journalists and pundits (along with everyone else who was paying attention) noticed that 2016 was a year when the world lost a huge number of icons and celebrities. It seemed like every day brought a new dose of celebrity death. Among those we lost: George Martin, George Kennedy, Harper Lee, Maurice White, Paul Kantner, Abe Vigoda, Glenn Frey, Dan Haggerty, Alan Rickman, Brian Bedford, David Bowie, Prince, Muhammad Ali, Phife Dawg, Garry Shandling, Florence Henderson, Alan Thicke, Gene Wilder, Arnold Palmer, Leonard Cohen, Patty Duke, Zsa Zsa Gabor, and, in the last week of the year, George Michael, Carrie Fisher (which I still haven't recovered from), and, twenty-four hours later, her mother, Debbie Reynolds. While some of them were expected (poor Abe Vigoda was the subject of a website called IsAbeVigodaDead.com that basically answered the question "no" every day until he died), many were utterly shocking and devastating.

On the morning after Bowie died, before I knew, my boyfriend asked, "Did something happen to David Bowie? He's all over Instagram."

I said, "It was his birthday on Friday and he has a new album."

"No," he said, "there are broken hearts. I think he died."

"No," I said quickly in disbelief. As sure as I was it wasn't possible, the idea made me frantic and a little nauseated. It didn't take long to find out it was true. And it seemed that Bowie knew when it was coming and prepared for it, and in a sense prepared us for it, if that's possible.

A new term was bandied about at the time: "cybermourning." Every day I looked on social media I saw people changed their avatars to his picture or the Bowie bolt of lightning, and they posted hundreds of articles, videos, photos, and reminiscences. Some were from people who knew Bowie, while most were from people who'd been moved and changed by him and his music. And the only thing that brought a slowing was the possibly even more shocking death of Prince. When I saw a post on Instagram with a picture of Prince that read "Not again! #RIP," I simply said, "No." No, no, no, no, no. The stages of grieving a celebrity are the same as grieving a regular person, except it's louder, faster, and public.

Cybermourning is a new concept, but the mourning of celebrities is as old as time. The Egyptians and Mayans built colossal monuments to worship their royal celebs; the Greeks and Romans organized massive funerals to commemorate poets and military heroes. In the 19th century the streets of Paris were filled with Victor Hugo's mourners when the great writer died.

And of course millions of us remember when Princess Diana died in 1997, the collective grief that surrounded the "People's Princess," and the glut of merchandise that appeared with her face on it.

What is it about their deaths that hits us so profoundly? I believe that in many ways these people are our gods and goddesses, beings in our midst that we don't think of as "just like us," even when they are. We watch them to escape and think of them as separate from time, even immortal, and in some ways they are: through film and TV and their recordings and writings. We feel that they are always supposed to be with us, making us feel happy or excited or engaged, but always better. It feels that with money and connections, someone should be able to be saved or preserved. Certainly people like James Gandolfini, who was only fifty-one, and Philip Seymour Hoffman, who died at forty-six, make us feel that we'd just gotten to know them. We weren't ready to lose them—nor are we ready to lose most celebrities when they die.

When Bowie died, there was a minor hubbub because a journalist tweeted how sickening it was that people mourned a stranger in this way. Her opinion was that people who didn't know him personally should give up their right to grieve. She pretty much got her head handed to her via social media, especially when someone found her earlier tweet about Michael Jackson dying and that she was going to take the rest of the week off.

Aside from being insensitive to the feelings of millions of people mourning Bowie's death, she was wrong. Who can say what a person has the right to feel sad about? A friend of mine, the writer Mira Jacob, was the first person I thought about when

Prince died because we'd worked together on the show *Pop-Up Video* and she had popped "When Doves Cry." She said she had noticed online that people were almost apologetic about their grief, because they didn't "know" Prince. She called BS.

"You never held Prince," she said. "So what? The way he spoke to you, the way he shaped and transformed you into someone you couldn't have imagined, was as vital as any relationship you will ever have . . . loving and grieving a man we never touched, that is us at our very best. No apology necessary."

There have been plenty of public figures who've died that I have barely batted an eyelash about, and others whose passing utterly broke my heart. I'm not always sure who is going to elicit a reaction either.

M attie and I talked about it. We broke it down into the surprise deaths, someone you just hadn't thought about dying, and the people who you always thought would be there, older, perennial perhaps, as she put it, in "the fabric of your life."

"I think Elvis Presley was my first," she recalled, "But then no one hit me more than Johnny Carson." Because like millions of people, she had spent every night with him for thirty years.

The surprise deaths are what she called the "if only" deaths: actors Paul Walker and Natalie Wood, for example, and news anchor Bob Simon.

Some psychologists believe this grief is all about transference. You couldn't really get in touch with your sadness when your uncle died, so it all came pouring out for, say, Jim Henson. While there's truth to that, there's transference in everything.

But it's also true that a person's art or presence means something to each of us, whether you lost your virginity to the strains of "Desperado," or dealt with the uncertainties in childhood helped by Kermit the Frog, or remember your dad laughing hysterically at Harvey Korman on *The Carol Burnett Show*. It's all real. The same as it's real to cry at a sad novel or movie.

Also, as a person who's been in therapy for eighty thousand years, I know that our strong reactions to anything can be useful in understanding ourselves. In 2011, I saw on Twitter that the musician Gerry Rafferty had died. "Baker Street," his biggest hit, is one of my favorite songs. Whenever I listen to it, it always takes me back to a time and place—being eleven in the summer of 1978, hanging with my brothers at the pool, feeling the explosive and probably hormonal excitement of what my life might one day become. In 2011, my life was not in a great place, and hearing those lyrics when Rafferty died made me feel homesick, nostalgic, and lost.

It is under debate whether the "viral mourning" that has occurred since the advent of the internet and social media is healthy. I think this comes from the psychological evidence that it was really not good for people to watch the events of 9/11 over and over again. And obviously if a person cannot function normally from too much cybermourning, they should seek help. But for those of us who may take comfort in knowing that there are others out there, strangers, who are feeling the way we feel, to me that can only be good. When Glenn Frey died and I saw that people posted great Eagles live performances on Facebook, it made me sad, but I took solace in the fact this communal remembrance of Frey with others felt good.

In a larger sense, though, I think this kind of collective mourning demonstrates our capacity to feel empathy, sadness, and the loss of someone we cared about whose talent—whether on a screen, a playing field, or a stage or in government—matters to us a lot.

Intermission 14

We had just landed at O'Hare. My father was at the luggage belt, waiting, with that thousand-yard stare. You could not interact with him at such times. He was hunting. I wandered away. Near the Avis counter, I ran into Muhammad Ali. He was just standing there, so it seemed to me. I said, "Hey, Champ." I was maybe eight. He got on a knee and goofed with me, called me "pretty boy" and threw fake haymakers. I went back and told my father, still at the belt, that I'd met the Champ. He said, "Yeah, yeah, luggage!" I went away again, sadly. Ali saw me. "Hey, pretty boy, what's wrong?" "My father doesn't believe I met you." Ali picked me up, held me against his ribs, and walked over. "Where is he?" I pointed him out. Ali walked over, raised his fist, in a funny way, then tapped my father on the shoulder. When my father turned around, there was Muhammad Ali, with a fist in his—my father's—face, saying, "My friend says you don't believe in me."

—RICH COHEN

★

*My parents had taken us children—my older sister and me—
to St. Croix, in the US Virgin Islands, for our school vacation. They had friends who owned a run-down hotel in the
center of Christiansted, the capital city. The hotel itself was
ostentatiously dilapidated, meaning that if you weren't able
to see the charm and history in cracking furniture and moldy
umbrellas and wall-to-wall discomfort, you probably didn't
belong there.*

*My parents, sister, and I and a few other people were
eating lunch under a dirty green-and-white umbrella by
the side of the pool one afternoon when twenty feet away
from us, a mother and son took a seat at a center table.
"Lauren Bacall," someone at the table said about the beautiful, slightly cruel-looking blond woman with the arresting
lipstick, and everyone agreed the blond boy with her was her
son, maybe by Jason Robards? Was his name Sam, maybe?*

*At the time I didn't know Lauren Bacall from Little
Lotta. If a famous person wasn't a Brady or a Partridge, I
wasn't interested. I was soon set straight by the adults that
Lauren Bacall was a famous film actress, linked by marriage
and by movies I'd never seen with Humphrey Bogart, and I
had, of course, heard of him.*

*My father was an English teacher, and sometime over
the course of his career it seemed he had taught Humphrey
Bogart and Lauren Bacall's older son, Stephen. A few minutes later, he wandered over to Lauren Bacall's table and
struck up a conversation with her.* How incredibly annoying

for her, *I remember thinking,* and how embarrassing for me. *Still, the conversation seemed to go well enough. At least Lauren Bacall didn't tear his head off, which I later found out she was fully capable of doing.*

For the rest of the lunch, it was hard to take my eyes away. The two of them, mother and son, appeared to be enveloped in some sexy, radiant, Christlike light. Yes, it had something to do with them, but it had more to do with us, the people watching and whispering and judging and admiring. At the time—I was twelve—I liked almost nothing about myself. I had taken to wearing articles of clothing I believed could fool other people into believing I was cool, tough, a ruffian of sorts. My first day in Christiansted I bought a T-shirt that read "Cruisin' with Cruzan Rum," so that back at school, my classmates, who I must have taken for idiots, would realize they had underestimated me, that I was in fact tough and dangerous, a charismatic, frequently drunk ne'er-do-well.

This is why instead of focusing on Lauren Bacall, I studied her son, who was famous by association in that strange celebrity way. He wore a double-breasted blue blazer and white pants with a sharp crease in them. He looked dashing and confident, exactly the way I imagined a movie star's son should and, it turned out, did dress. I had never seen anyone wearing a double-breasted blue blazer before. The one or two I owned had the usual three buttons along one side, and holes on the other.

Once they had picked up and left, the world suddenly seemed disappointing—smaller, crummier, less possible.

Even with the sun hot and bright, it felt as though a lot of the light and beauty in the world had been sucked away, despite the fact that five minutes earlier I'd never even heard of Lauren Bacall. I knew they had disappeared forever, and I actually felt bereft. Surely they were staying someplace vastly better than where we were, some modern, towering place with comfortable furniture, lamps that actually turned on, and no drunks in the lobby. The gold buttons on Sam Robards's coat—they were like eyes in the dark, and they still gleam in my brain today. In my ongoing efforts to distract the world from the person I was, and disliked, I knew I would do everything in my power when I got home to score a double-breasted blue blazer.

Over the next few weeks after vacation, I badgered my mother to buy me a double-breasted blue blazer. For a long time she said no, before finally caving in. When I tried it on for the first time, it looked ridiculous. I looked exactly like the person I was trying to escape from—me—except now my self-hatred was on display alongside my attempt to disguise that person. Instead of looking like Sam Robards, I looked like the head of hospitality on some sinking cruise ship. The same went for my "Cruisin' with Cruzan Rum" T-shirt, which, outside the Virgin Islands and doubtlessly inside, too, made me look like a complete moron.

—PETER SMITH

FIFTEEN

FADE OUT

★

We have always looked to our famous people for entertainment, example, and escape, but we are now living in a time when access to information and direct
contact has dialed the interest level up to 11. Why? You open up
Google and you can find out about a great scientific stride made
by a cancer researcher or a video of a never-before-seen tribe
in New Guinea, yet you input "Jennifer Lawrence response to
nude photos leak."

While thinking about this question, I distracted myself by
watching my favorite Hollywood films. One of them is *Sullivan's
Travels*. Considered one of director Preston Sturges's greatest
films, it is the story of John Sullivan (played by the magnificent
Joel McCrea), a successful movie director of popular come-
dies. He's become weary of cinematic silliness and wants to

make a socially conscious movie about the downtrodden common man, "a true canvas of the suffering of humanity," pretentiously titled O *Brother, Where Art Thou?* Of course the studio heads hate the idea. They want him to make another light-hearted comedy. But Sullivan talks them into letting him try. He decides to dress as a hobo (even carrying one of those bandanna bundles tied to a stick) to learn about trouble firsthand. The studio heads, wanting to protect their investment, send along with him a caravan of all the modern, luxurious conveniences (food, liquor, a hot shower, and support personnel). Sullivan pays them off to leave him alone and sets out on his own to hitchhike—badly. He ends up back in Los Angeles, where he meets the Girl (played by the gorgeous Veronica Lake), an actress who is about to quit show business and believes Sullivan really is a tramp, so she makes him ham and eggs. To repay her kindness, Sullivan takes her back to his manse to get his car and give her a lift. Though she's furious at him for deceiving her, she ends up becoming his traveling companion. They make another failed attempt at becoming hoboes and finally Sullivan succeeds in living like a hobo, sort of. They end up in a Hooverville, eating food scraps and being deloused. It's no longer for show. He decides for the sake of the girl to call it quits on his experiment, and the studio publicizes it as a huge success. The Girl wants to stay with him, but she can't because he's married. (But not for love, of course: on the advice of his business manager, Sullivan had gotten married to reduce his income tax. Ironically, he discovers that his wife cost him double what he saved in taxes. Women!)

Sullivan decides to help the homeless by handing out five thousand dollars in five-dollar bills to all the tramps he meets, and he does it in his hobo clothes. But one man decides he wants more than his share and he ambushes Sullivan, taking the cash and Sullivan's shoes. Sullivan is knocked unconscious and is thrown into a boxcar on its way out of town. The thief ends up dropping the loose cash on the rails and then is run over and killed by another train while picking it up. When the thief's body is found, they discover a special card in his shoes, misidentifying him as Sullivan. The mangled body is assumed to be Sullivan's, and his staff and the Girl are informed of his death. Meanwhile, Sullivan wakes up in a rail yard in another city, with no memory of who he is or how he got there. (Amnesia is a much bigger issue in Hollywood than in life.) In his confused state, he assaults the railroad worker who finds him, is caught, and is sentenced to six years in a labor camp. While there, Sullivan slowly regains his memory. To entertain the prisoners, the wardens show some movies. Noticing the pure joy in the faces of his fellow inmates—the audience—Sullivan realizes that comedy can do more good for the poor than can O Brother, Where Art Thou?

But Sullivan still has a problem: he cannot convince anybody he is the movie director John Sullivan. Finally, he comes up with an ingenious solution: he confesses to being his own killer. When his picture makes the front page of the newspapers, the Girl recognizes him and gets him released. His "widow" had already taken up with his crooked business manager, so he can now divorce her and reunite with the Girl. The studio says he can make *O Brother, Where Art Thou?* but he says no, he can't. He's too happy in his personal life, thanks to the Girl. And he hasn't suffered enough to make the movie.

The movie was released in January 1942, the month after December 1941, when the Japanese bombed Pearl Harbor and America entered World War II. People's lives were suddenly turned upside down. Everything was different. Uncertain and downright scary. At the end of the film, Sullivan poignantly remarks, "There's a lot to be said for making people laugh! Did you know that's all some people have? It isn't much, but it's better than nothing in this cockeyed caravan!"

So *Sullivan's Travels* was my answer to why we choose to watch celebrities. Though I think Sullivan is wrong when he says, "It isn't much, but it's better than nothing." I think it's quite a lot. And I prepared to write my findings.

As I was finishing this book, I got an email from my daughter's teacher. The subject line was "Failing Health," which I thought was kind of an old-fashioned expression for the teacher to use to describe her condition. Except the teacher wasn't in failing health; my daughter was failing health class. Her only pass/fail course. At the time she was in seventh grade, which is the grade that New York City high school admissions people look at when choosing students. Apparently seventh grade can either make you the next head of Universal Pictures or send you packing to the Triangle Shirtwaist Factory.

I dropped everything I was doing and started to help my daughter make up a semester's worth of homework that she'd somehow lost.

Unfortunately, after helping her with her work, I didn't want to go back to finish writing this book.

One afternoon I was walking my dogs and I passed a news-stand and I saw a brand-new issue of *Harper's Bazaar*, and who was on the cover? Why, Jennifer Aniston! I snapped it up, eager to get home and dive in.

I learned firsthand my own lesson in the value of celebrity culture as escapism. Watching them, reading about them, is a way to take us out of our doldrums and into another place; it doesn't cost much and it can be less than five minutes, but we are out of here. The reasons we are obsessed with them are many, and the celebrities we like are our gods: we look up to them as examples of what we want to do. And even when they are just like us, they are not us: they are more beautiful, more talented, more athletic, more impressive—they are the us we want to be. And for those moments when we are with them—in a theater seat, at the ballpark, at a concert—we can take a break from being us, too. It doesn't last forever and may not be a lot, but sometimes that's enough.

INTERMISSION BIOS

Esther Newberg is an executive vice president at ICM and co-chair of its New York office, and lucky to be Julie Klam's agent.

Mary Testa is an award-winning stage and film actress and singer.

Cathi Hanauer is the *New York Times*–bestselling author of three novels and two essay anthologies, most recently *The Bitch Is Back: Older, Wiser, and (Getting) Happier*.

Jen Deaderick is working on a cartoon history of the Equal Rights Amendment.

Sascha Rothchild is a film and television writer. Her memoir, *How to Get Divorced by 30*, was published by Penguin. She has also been featured on *This American Life*. She lives in Los Angeles with two dogs and one husband.

Jancee Dunn has written six books and lives in Brooklyn.

Laura Zigman is the author of four novels and several uncredited works of "collaborative nonfiction" (ghostwriting).

Jeff Fisher works in television and currently creates, produces, and directs television and digital content.

Mae Martin is the cofounder of AIM House and Madelife. She lives in Boulder, Colorado, with her husband and four kids.

Lydia Butler has been a teacher and an elementary school librarian since time began. Although she has many interesting friends, she herself is not very interesting.

Harry Shearer is an actor, voice actor, comedian, writer, musician, author, radio host, director, and producer.

Patricia Marx often gets mistaken for British royalty (all of them).

Kelly Carlin is an author, speaker, podcaster, SiriusXM radio host, and general rabble-rouser.

Alec Sokolow is a nonpracticing atheist from the Upper West Side of New York City who went to an Episcopal school where he was never fondled—not even by himself. He was kicked out of summer camp for staging an anti-color war rally. Later, when the Communist Party rejected him, he joined the Writers Guild of America.

Adriana Trigiani is a writer who lives in Greenwich Village with her family.

Merrill Stubbs is a native New Yorker, mother of two, and cofounder of Food52, which brings millions of people together to eat thoughtfully and live joyfully.

Alan Smithee is the official pseudonym used by film directors who wish to disown a project (in other words, it's not his real name).

Robbie Kondor is an award-winning composer, pianist, studio musician, and producer living in New York.

Lee Woodruff is a *New York Times*–bestselling author and journalist who retired from celebrity stalking after her first pregnancy.

Marisa Acocella Marchetto is a *New York Times*–bestselling graphic author who lives in New York City.

Ann Leary is a *New York Times*–bestselling author of *The Good House, The Children, Outtakes from a Marriage,* and *An Innocent, a Broad.*

Julie Gold is a Grammy Award–winning songwriter best known for penning Bette Midler's worldwide anthem "From a Distance."

Claudia Glaser-Mussen is a psychotherapist in private practice and a musician in the Grammy-nominated band Brady Rymer and the Little Band That Could. She has a dog that is more handsome than George Clooney and she has a fear of ventriloquists, blue cheese, and snakes.

Kate Christensen is a PEN/Faulkner Award–winning writer who lives in Maine.

Gail Dosik is a cake and cookie maker and dog lover in New York City.

Tara Dublin is a writer, single mom, and media personality in Portland, Oregon.

Allison Winn Scotch is the *New York Times*–bestselling author of six novels and lives in Los Angeles with her family and their dogs.

Cathy Ladman is a comedian, actor, and writer, including of her solo show *Does This Show Make Me Look Fat?*

Ted Travelstead writes for television and movies, and sometimes acts in them.

AJ Mendez Brooks is a former pro-wrestling champion, animal rights activist, and the author of *Crazy Is My Superpower*.

Marcia Klam is an energy healer who in her spare time works for the Democratic Party. She has been married for fifty-seven years and has three children, one of whom is really excellent, and four grandchildren, all of whom are really excellent.

Kera Bolonik is a writer and the executive editor of *Dame* magazine.

Paul Leo is a writer and producer living in New York City.

Gigi Levangie Grazer is a mom, screenwriter (*Stepmom*), novelist (*The Starter Wife, Maneater, The After Wife*), and a cautious optimist. Fan of sweat.

Rich Cohen is a bestselling author and journalist.

Peter Smith is a novelist, journalist, and ghostwriter.

ACKNOWLEDGMENTS

This was the only book I ever turned in late for a confluence of really good reasons, and I have so many people to thank for pulling me out of my local OTB and helping me get it done.

I have been, as the celebrities say, #blessed to have had Esther Newberg as an agent and friend for five books (and counting). She is beautiful, brave, benevolent, and she scares all the right people. I love her and couldn't and wouldn't do anything without her.

Geoff Kloske, a well-known titan of the publishing industry, was such a mensch. He never once sent a henchman after me, and when I admitted to ducking him because my manuscript was so late, he told me, "I've got bigger problems than you." Sniff sniff, I love you, Geoff!

Jake Morrissey, the editor every writer dreams of, came into this game with two outs, bottom of the ninth, and he hit a grand slam. Jake, it would take a whole book for me to properly thank you for pulling this together, encouraging me, and making me feel like faking my death instead of writing the book was a bad idea. Thank God for you, the wind beneath my wings.

Enormous thanks to my Riverhead family: Claire McGinnis, Jynne Dilling Martin, Kate Stark, Lydia Hirt, Kevin Murphy, Liz Hohenadel, and Katie Freeman. My gifted copy editor, M. P. Klier; the legal genius Karen Mayer; and my former Riverhead editor but always friend Megan Lynch.

I am eternally grateful to the people who took the time to let me interview them when I was starstruck and tongue-tied. Dearest Timothy Hutton, Griffin Dunne, Michael Black, Julie Warner, R. A. Dickey, Isabel Gillies, Bumble Ward, Jon Ronson, Deborah Copaken, Lynda Obst, Ned Van Zandt, Paul Myers, Dr. Lisa Weinstock, and Harry Shearer.

I was lucky enough to sit down with the late Doris Roberts at her dining room table and chat about celebrity. She was lovely and I am grateful to have met her.

My aunt Mattie Smith Matthews was not only a hugely important source for intangible material, but she bought me lots of boozy lunches and told me everything was going to be OK when I panicked, which was a lot.

Thank you to everyone I am lucky enough to call a friend. You all had to hear about this book way more then you wanted. Laura Zigman, Ann Leary, Claudia Glaser-Mussen, Patty Marx, Meg Wolitzer, Gigi Levangie Grazer, Jancee Dunn, Barbara Warnke, Caitlin McNiff, Adam Resnick, Jeanette Benzie, Martha Broderick, Agnes Wilkie, Vesna Jovanovic, Diane Sokolow, Kristin Moavenian, Mira Jacob, Susan Roxborough, Judith Newman, Kera Bolonik, Mae Martin, Molly Jong-Fast, and Peter Smith.

Bouquets of roses to everyone who answered my plea for their brushes with celebrity.

Love love love to my family especially my mom (MOMMY!!!) and dad; my brothers, Heckle and Jeckle; Ellie Rose Davenport; and my sweet little Violet flower.

I already dedicated this whole book to you, Dan Davenport, but I just love you so so so so much.

During the writing of this book, my dear, sweet friend Lisa Bonchek Adams died of cancer. She helped me figure out a million things and I miss her desperately. This book was written in her loving memory.